T0160227

ALIGN

CHRIS MEROFF

ALIGN

Four Simple Steps for Leaders to Create Employee ~~Engagement~~ *Fulfillment*

NEW YORK

LONDON • NASHVILLE • MELBOURNE • VANCOUVER

Align

Four Simple Steps for Leaders to Create Employee ~~Engagement~~ Fulfillment

© 2021 Chris Meroff

All rights reserved. No portion of this book may be reproduced, stored in a retrieval system, or transmitted in any form or by any means—electronic, mechanical, photocopy, recording, scanning, or other—except for brief quotations in critical reviews or articles, without the prior written permission of the publisher.

Published in New York, New York, by Morgan James Publishing. Morgan James is a trademark of Morgan James, LLC. www.MorganJamesPublishing.com

ISBN 9781642799941 paperback
ISBN 9781642799958 eBook
Library of Congress Control Number: 2020930827

Cover & Interior Design by:
Christopher Kirk
www.GFSstudio.com

Illustrations by:
Blah Blah Media

Morgan James is a proud partner of Habitat for Humanity Peninsula and Greater Williamsburg. Partners in building since 2006.

Get involved today! Visit
MorganJamesPublishing.com/giving-back

*For my kids: May your workplace experience be shaped
by the principles in this book and may they help you
use your God-given gifts and talents to their fullest.*

TABLE OF CONTENTS

Step Three: Create Value

Step Four: Create Success

FOREWORD

As I write the foreword to this book, the entire globe is right in the middle of a global pandemic caused by COVID-19. I mention this at the outset because no matter who you are or what time in history you are reading this book, you will be aware of this event. It is so significant that it either has or will impact every human being on the planet in some way, shape, or form. It is the first time in my lifetime that the entire globe has had one common goal, to "flatten the curve." All of humanity is trying to fight the coronavirus and stop the spread. It is a noble goal and an important one because it affects all of us, and it is a matter of life and death.

Similarly, all of humanity, at some point in their lives, comes into contact with some employment, work, job, or task. Most of us will spend the vast majority of our waking adult hours tied up in some employment. All of us, whether we are willing to accept it or not, can shape that experience for ourselves and others to either be a positive or negative experience. Unfortunately, the statistics show that the vast majority of people who come into contact with work don't enjoy what they do and don't find fulfillment. The dissatisfaction often comes from their work environment, not the work they do. Many factors play into this, but with the curve of unfulfilled workers being so high, I think we should all make it our goal to flatten the curve of employee dissatisfaction in our lifetime. To stop the spread of being dissatisfied with our work and workplaces. All of us can stop the trend no matter what your role is in the organization where you work. The fact that you are reading this book suggests that you may have a desire to see that curve flatten for yourself and others. But just like coronavirus, you can't blame others for the spread. You have to take responsibility for your part and lead, starting with yourself. Thankfully you don't have to figure out how to flatten the curve of employee dissatisfaction on your own. My friend, Chris Meroff, has put together an incredible guide for you on how to do it. As you read this book, you will discover that it starts with you first before you can help others.

I first met Chris Meroff in the Summer of 2002 in the tiny coastal town of Machiasport, Maine, USA. Eventually, I went to work for his family's business two years later, and we worked together for more than a decade. The stories of adventure I experienced in working with Chris are so many it would fill more than a dozen books of this size. As I write this from tropical Queensland, Australia, I am laughing out loud as I recall some of those adventures. From the very beginning of my relationship with Chris, I experienced two of his most exceptional qualities as a leader, his generosity and loyalty. His care for people shines through in these qualities, which I have experienced time and time again. Once, on a flight from Boise, Idaho to Denver, Colorado, I had a medical emergency. The next twenty-four hours would be one of the scariest and most unsettling times in my life. Chris was a loyal and generous friend throughout the whole experience. For the next nine months in the workplace, as I was trying to figure out what was wrong with me physically, his generosity and loyalty never stopped. It is no surprise to me that he has developed a personal mission to eliminate employee dissatisfaction from the workplaces where he leads. It is his generous spirit that motivates him to pass this on to others for their benefit also. Chris has not stumbled upon these truths easily; in fact, quite the contrary. I know it was through much trial, error, heartache, and victory that these truths developed. Chris would be the first to tell you much of this book has been written out of failure and finally some success. It is because of the road he has traveled that I believe Chris is so rightly positioned to share these insights with you, the reader.

If you are anything like me, you may pick up this book with the need for a slight perspective adjustment, so may I give you a word of warning before you begin reading. My wife, Kristin, and I once read a parenting book that transformed our family. When we first set out to read the book, we thought the author was going to give us all of the things we could change about our children. What we quickly discovered was that the most significant change that needed to take place was with us. So it is with leadership and employee fulfillment. You may be thinking this book will help you radically change the way your employees feel about your workplace. This statement is true to some extent; however, as you will discover, that will most likely come through your transformation, not theirs. I hope you are willing to journey through this process. I think you are up to it, and I am confident that you will be glad you went on the journey. The practical applications in this book is what sets it apart from other leadership books I have read. I would suggest working through the content with others in your organization, whether paid or unpaid team members. Don't head out on the journey alone! *Align* is not just a book about leadership theories. It is a practical, hands-on approach to revolutionizing your workplace culture. It is filled with great questions to ask of yourself and your organization, along with a real-life case study on how these principles can impact a life.

Writer Annie Dillard famously said, "How we spend our days is, of course, how we spend our lives." For many of us, a large portion of our days are at work; in fact, the average person will spend 90,000 hours at work over a lifetime. It's safe to say then; your job can make a significant impact on your quality of life. That's why the principles written by my friend Chris Meroff are so timely and essential no matter who you are and when you are reading this book. Here is my hope and prayer for you as you read this book: that it will transform both your journey to employee fulfillment and the lives of everyone you have the privilege of working alongside. That's been my experience, and I believe it can be yours too.

Cheers,
Jason 'Perko' Perkins

Fulfillment

Fulfillment is a deep satisfaction
in accomplishment through
the development of your
inherent character.

INTRODUCTION

When you picked up this book you might have been thinking, "Will this give me a realistic plan to be a successful leader?" I get it. I wanted the same. Only a few years ago I would have thought that as well. I am an avid reader and consumer of books, especially books that inspire and teach me. I was growing frustrated with books in the leadership space.

But then something interesting happened. The organization that I built began to challenge my thinking and long-held beliefs about leadership. For example, I had always heard (and believed) that leaders are born, not made. But I found that leaders can be made if you create the right incubator and environment. When we did that, leaders in my organization began to surface. And not just leaders, great leaders! My first reaction to this phenomenon was shock.

We were growing rapidly, and I needed great leaders. And there they were—right in front of me.

My second reaction was to do what I always do: Question it. I began to take a deep dive into what was happening and here's what I discovered: The system itself was producing leaders, creating them and equipping them, at a much higher rate than I could have imagined. When my focus changed from searching for leaders to creating the kind of workplace that inspires people to lead, success happened.

Like most of us, I want to win. More importantly, I absolutely hate to lose! Having the right leaders in my organization assured me of winning every single day. The numbers proved it. The joy in the workplace proved it. The team's sense of purpose, laser focus, and creativity proved it. The diverse group of leaders, regardless of age, gender, or background, proved it.

My third reaction was to write this book and share it with you. I realized this philosophy worked for everyone involved in my organization and therefore could work anywhere and with any leader willing to love and serve people toward fulfillment.

That's it—that's leadership: loving and serving people.

What happened in my organization when I implemented what you will read in these pages surprised even me. In my case, leaders who didn't even know they were leaders and who didn't necessarily aspire to it when they were hired on grew and became their best selves. They found the one thing they do better than anyone else—their leadership superpower. That gave them leadership fulfillment. They finally understood what the sacrifice of leadership was all about and it was already written on their hearts. While most people go to work every day and struggle through, these people came alive, coming in early, filled with enthusiasm and innovation, all in an effort to love and serve people.

If you love your people, it doesn't get any better than that.

We are going to spend the rest of this book unwrapping this philosophy. Here's what you'll find. If you think that leadership is only about you, then you'll be confused by what I am proposing. If you think that leadership is about a position or title, then I will lose you on this journey to leadership fulfillment.

However, if you want your people to find fulfillment, which is a deep satisfaction in achievement and accomplishment through the development of one's inherent character, then this book is for you. You will find what I have found. This philosophy is a revolution created out of necessity.

I want people to find their value. I want people to know they are leaders and so I created a company that gives you or your organization the best chance to make this a reality. I can promise you the effort is well worth it.

So how are we doing? Are you with me?

Chapter 1

BEGIN AT THE BEGINNING

I am a leadership failure … and I am proud of it.

My management learning curve has been long and brutal, to say the least. I have spent lots of time and money hiring shiny people and programs that I was certain would take my organization to the next level, only to find somewhere down the road that they were a terrible fit for our company. After running up against that brick wall over and over again, I made a discovery that changed everything. I created an aligned workplace where leaders would choose me instead of the other way around. You should try it. Let me help you shortcut the learning curve.

This shortcut extends beyond the workplace. If something is true, it has to be true all the time. I raised my kids in a typical household where the command-and-control style of parenting was how things got done. I didn't understand the importance of things like purpose, fulfillment, culture, or alignment.

Applying healthy tension and addressing those things that no one wants to talk about are integral to fulfillment, and fulfillment is key to effective leadership.

I've learned that work isn't just about responsibilities, tasks, and projects. There are people involved. People typically do not like being dictated to, but they love having a say in the work they do. They love doing work that aligns with their hopes and dreams, knowing they're working for a greater purpose. They love knowing their coworkers and their leaders believe in them, support them, and want them to succeed.

Communicating clear expectations and following up on them may feel weird to you at first. You might think you're ill-equipped to handle it. These conversations may feel awkward or uncomfortable, but you can learn how to have them. Don't avoid them because they are difficult. Like riding a bike, you may fall a time or two, but eventually you'll get the hang of it. In this series of books, I will share with you what I have found to work best. But remember that people are people, and people are complicated. Don't try to lay one template that you learned in a book over your organization and try to use it exactly the way we do here. Adapt it. Use what does work for you and discard the rest.

You don't have to be great at it. You don't even have to be good at it to start with. You just have to be willing to ask the right questions and listen intently to the answers, because without these conversations, you and your people will never be aligned, and you will never enjoy the incredible benefits this philosophy can bring.

Let me tell you a story about my friend, Kyle, and his journey from discontentment to true employee fulfillment.

Kyle's Story

Kyle grew up in a home deeply rooted in the value of service to others. His mother, a math teacher by trade, taught Kyle how to gracefully lead people and adapt his level of support to fit each individual's unique journey. Through her tireless personal investment into those she felt called to care for, she consistently demonstrated how to best serve each person by simply seeing them for who they are. Regardless of whether this happened through her work in teaching, Kyle learned that she found value and fulfillment in seeking others.

Kyle's father, a pastor, showed him how to serve his community as a whole by pursuing people in their times of need, even when they weren't aware they even needed help. The relationships he cultivated with his community fostered the idea that giving back really served *everyone*. Visiting the sick in the hospital or chatting with the elderly in their homes or even just getting on a first-name basis with local store employees illustrated the importance of connections to all, not just those with whom we share things in common. Although his father's role as a pastor called on him to connect with those in his church, Kyle recognized that his father found fulfillment through his relationships to the wider community.

Kyle's parents' skill sets complemented the other and, through their partnership, they led all their children, including Kyle, with both actions and words. Every morning before school, Kyle's dad would tell him and his siblings that they must lead by example. "You don't have to be the loudest, you don't have to be perfect, but people will see what you do." His powerful words coupled with their family's solid foundations and principles led Kyle to understand that fulfillment was not just possible—it was attainable *and* a necessary component to life.

Once Kyle began working in a field similar to his father's, he expected to find that same sense of fulfillment he saw in his family life. The organization he worked for claimed one purpose but, in reality, was living out and acting on another. Kyle felt a disconnect and couldn't understand why his employment, though aligned with his experience and values, didn't match up to what he was getting from his workplace culture. He felt lost and went home feeling unfulfilled every day. He didn't yet understand that what he was seeking was alignment.

Kyle's situation isn't unusual. In fact, over 70 percent of people in America don't feel fulfilled by their work.[1*]

Think about that for a moment. That means at least two out of every three people you see at work are unfulfilled. Like Kyle, they come into a job with high hopes for a fulfilling career, but somewhere along the line they become disconnected from the purpose of the company or role. Or maybe they never felt that connection at all.

I don't blame Kyle. Like many people, he wanted to win, but there was no structure and no path in place that allowed him to do that. The leadership in his organization never created that structure or developed the path he needed to feel fulfilled. Think about the people who come to work for you. Think about how excited they are in their interviews and during those initial weeks when they're learning the job and getting to know everyone. They're passionate and want so much to succeed, but then something happens over time. Without the leadership in place to teach them how to fight for fulfillment, they'll leave to pursue fulfillment elsewhere. And rightfully so. People have intrinsic value and are entitled to fulfillment.

I don't blame Kyle's leadership. I know firsthand what leaders go through and how difficult it can be to build a

---

1 *Marcel Schwantes, "A New Study Reveals 70 Percent of Workers Say They Are Actively Looking for a New Job. Here's the Reason in 5 Words," *Inc,* December 4, 2018, accessed March 28, 2019, https://www.inc.com/marcel-schwantes/a-new-study-reveals-70-percent-of-workers-say-they-areactively-looking-for-a-new-job-heres-reason-in-5-words.html

company and develop a team that feels like they're winning every day. I struggled for years, but now I can look back at those challenges and understand how they prevented me from leadership success. I learned how to overcome them with aligning, which ultimately helped Kyle's journey to fulfillment.

The Leadership Struggle

Leaders may have good intentions but fall short of creating employee fulfillment and ultimately achieving true alignment. You may be going through this yourself and wondering why leading seems so difficult. You're not alone. The leadership struggle is more common than you think, and the symptoms are many.

Common Symptoms of the Leadership Struggle

- Ambiguous company purpose
- Misalignment between people and company/team/individual purpose
- Instability during times of crisis
- Lack of commitment to core values
- Lack of cohesion or feeling of togetherness among employees
- No personal or professional fulfillment

If you feel this struggle, trust me, your people are feeling it too. Your employees don't feel fulfilled, and over time, they'll leave your organization in search of fulfillment somewhere else, just like Kyle. High employee turnover is increasingly common, and though it's easy to blame the millennials or outside circumstances, the reality is that people of all generations and in all economies leave jobs because of misalignment. This happens when no one has truly and adequately defined how to win at work.

Misalignment also creates distance between you and your own leaders, because you feel like you're letting them down. You might even feel like you don't deserve your leadership position. This misalignment between you and your leaders—and you and your employees—creates incredible stress. And no one leaves stress at work. We take it home with us, where it affects our family life and other personal relationships.

I've written this book because I believe there is a way out of this cycle, but you must have the strength of will to go through it. To become the leader you were meant to be, the leader you have the gifts to be, you have to see enough value in getting out of the cycle to trade your comfort today for the kind of a leader you can become tomorrow. *Simple, not easy.*

I had done this and knew it was possible for anyone willing to take these steps. This is what I explained to Kyle when he first came to work with me. He had experienced many of these struggles and he wanted a job where he felt fulfilled. Once we talked about what he was going through and what he truly wanted for his career, I knew I could work with him. As long as he was open to fully comprehending and committing to alignment, Kyle could look forward to a bright future not only as an employee, but as a leader.

We'll circle back to Kyle's story and his journey throughout this book. These kinds of stories are fascinating to me and are incredibly fulfilling.

I know you're busy performing and achieving, wearing a lot of hats and falling into bed every night with nothing left in the tank. I get that. I've been there. And, now here comes another leadership book telling me that I need to overhaul what I do and how I do it. Will I even have time for that?

Are you with me?

This will take strength of will, and for that, you and I have to be aligned in our intentions. It's important for you to know that my definition of leadership is loving and serving people toward professional and personal fulfillment. To help you find the will to persevere through these steps, you need to redefine winning through that lens. If you define winning as a way to benefit only yourself, you won't have the strength of will to pull it off.

But if you accept the true meaning of winning as serving the success of others and, in turn, serving a purpose that's bigger than yourself, you will find the strength of will. You'll discover the bravery to have these conversations in a way that excites you. Are you prepared to make the transformation that empowers you to lead in a way that allows for true fulfillment? Are you ready to start winning?

Keep reading.
I want to talk to you about culture.

CREATE CULTURE

*Culture is the culmination of your people's hopes,
preferences, traditions, experiences, and beliefs.*

Chapter 2

YOUR CULTURE

*The individual traits of a person affect how they
view the world and interact with others.*

C ulture. We have all heard that word a lot, but what does it really mean? Culture is widely discussed but seldom defined in a way that's useful for the purpose of alignment. However, it's critical to understand the meaning of culture as it relates to this concept so you can learn how to cultivate it within your company. Creating a culture is the first step.

My definition of culture is *the sum of a group of people's hopes, preferences, traditions, experiences, and beliefs*. This is something I'll be repeating a lot throughout the book. And, let me be clear—every individual arrives at your workplace with their own unique and deeply held *hopes, preferences, traditions, experiences, and beliefs*. Once you understand this, you can no longer look at your workforce or your teams the same way. This individualistic view of your people is at the core of this philosophy and is critical to achieving it. Each person brings their unique self to your workplace every day to accomplish the purpose you have described to them and that they feel they're an integral part of. See your people through the lens of intrinsic value.

Any time you put people together, a culture is created. Whether or not you agree with each person's worldview—their *hopes, preferences, traditions, experiences, or beliefs*—that worldview exists, and you need to understand it. Remember, the effort to understand someone's worldview reflects your belief that they have intrinsic value. So, what works for one may not work for another. It's your job to solve that puzzle to assess and define what your culture is today.

This is complicated, and sometimes messy, but completely necessary. These days, people in the workplace want to be understood for who they really are. The old top-down, command-and-control style of management doesn't care about who you are or how you see the world. People have choices, and they will keep moving until they find fulfillment at work. They are not satisfied spending hours and hours away from their families to get a paycheck. They want both a paycheck and work that matters.

Misconceptions about Culture

Culture cannot be developed by simply creating environments where people congregate together. However, this is often a business's first step in creating a defined company culture. In my journey of leadership, this is a concept I fell prey to early on. In an effort to increase employee engagement, I created happy hours, pizza Fridays, and a party planning committee. What I didn't realize was that without the initial investment in people *before* creating these events that fostered community, the experience would, at best, be a shallow attempt at culture. Alignment requires an intimate pursuit of employees and this pursuit will never happen at a happy hour or a five-minute interaction while sharing a slice of pepperoni.

As I began to develop this theory of aligning, I realized the real win was much deeper—employee fulfillment. A happy hour can actually be an icebreaker to introduce someone into a community and begin to build a deeper relationship. It's the first step, or it can be. We leverage these opportunities to further discover the diversity in our employees to start a dialogue and really get to know them, which leads to alignment. Again, simple, not easy. If you want to develop a culture where you're able to authentically allow your employees to be known, heard, and valued, you'll have to take the necessary time and really listen.

Where to Start

Creating a culture starts with conversations between you

and your people to clearly define the culture you have—and the one you want to build together. You need to have conversations that clarify the culture of your team, the culture of your department, and the culture of the company. This needs to be perfectly understood both from the leader's perspective *and* the employees' perspective.

Creating a culture won't happen overnight. People's worldviews are deeply rooted in who they are and combining them into a culture that works for everyone will require people to make changes. And change is never easy. It rarely happens quickly. It takes time. It could take three years or longer for a culture to be created, cultivated, and bear plentiful fruit. This is no "flavor of the month" management exercise. This is an overhaul that leads to greatness and is worth the effort.

Throughout this book, I will tell the story of Kyle, a member of our leadership team and a truly remarkable person. Like all people, Kyle has his own journey that is uniquely his. He brings all of that to our company culture and we are better off for it. Who he is as a person and what he needs from work is based on his upbringing with his parents, the activities they did as a family serving the people of the community, and his established hopes, preferences, traditions, experiences, and beliefs. His parents, teachers, community, and church instilled a deeply held belief about how people should be treated, traditions of serving people in the community, preferences on how to serve people in need, and actual experiences of living out who his family is. Kyle longs to live out that tradition and make a difference in more lives. When he comes to the workplace, he is wanting, needing, desiring for his work experience to produce the same fulfillment that aligns with his worldview.

As a leader, it's my job to build an aligned culture that allows that to happen for Kyle, and we need to accomplish that together. He has a role to play in the process, and he can't just wait for me to do it all and let him know when it's done.

His work needs to take into account that need he has to serve. His role in our overall mission is vital, and I am certain that he is just the right person to carry it out. I know this because I know Kyle. Authentic conversations produce employee success, and this is a shining example of it.

Who are your "Kyles"? Have you identified them? Have you gotten to really know them?

Define Your Culture

Mission systems are critical to company culture. Your people must *believe* in the purpose of your company and its guiding principles. Belief is powerful. It directly affects how we act. Think about it like this: Out of all the traits that make up someone's worldview, belief is the only one powerful enough to start wars.

You can use the terms "mission" and "purpose" interchangeably. In my mind, they are one and the same. I prefer to use the term *purpose*, so throughout this book that is the word you will see. Feel free to insert *mission* there if that is better for you and clarifies our message for you.

Basically, purpose tells you where you're going, and guiding principles tell you how to act on your way to getting there. Both are essential to building an aligned culture. They are the template you lay down over every decision and you have to know them well and refer to them often to be sure that you are on track and aligned. We'll discuss guiding principles in more detail later on.

Before we move on, I'll just add this: When you define your culture, resist the urge to just adopt whatever's written on your company website. Early in my career, I created definitions of culture in a vacuum with senior management or human resources and without the input of all the employees. That exercise, not surprisingly, didn't accomplish much and may have even created some negative impact in my organization. Those of us who created the definitions understood them completely, but no one else did. I have learned from trial and many errors that this outcome is tragic, especially if you love your people. If culture in your organization is just a buzzword on a website, it means nothing. Without the people behind it, it's meaningless.

Lastly, you probably know that an ingrained culture already exists in your company—whether you created it intentionally or not. You have people. They bring what they bring to the workplace. That means there is some kind of culture somewhere along the spectrum from highly productive and beautiful to toxic and actively disengaged. The bottom line: Your culture may be close to the one you want, or it may be a long way off.

The good news is that you *can* improve it no matter where it is today.

_____

Chapter 2 Summary and Application

Often, under traditional leadership, a job feels like *work*. I wanted true fulfillment for my people, so they'd feel like they never have to work a day in their lives. Both you and your people need to be fulfilled to thrive, and that means making sure that time spent away from family every day is not worthless or even detrimental. You have to want—really *want*—to ensure everyone is in alignment to the culture so that each situation is a win-win for all involved.

Connect with your employees through a foundation of trust built on shared beliefs in a culture. Remember, culture starts with the sum of a group of people's hopes, preferences, traditions, experiences, and beliefs—their worldviews. Before you can begin building the culture you want, you need to start identifying the culture that already exists through each person's worldview. You have to know each individual in and out to understand how they align to the culture you have *and* the one you want. This takes time and effort. You have to care about your people to even undertake such a thing, but I can tell you firsthand that the outcomes will resonate far beyond the bottom line.

As you begin this transformational process to alignment, ask yourself these questions:

1. How would you define your company's culture? Take a moment to articulate how your company's culture is lived out.

2. What are the most noticeable gaps between the culture you currently have and the culture you want?

3. What benefits do you see in knowing the world-views—hopes, preferences, traditions, experiences, and beliefs—of the people you work with?

4. Who do you know the least? What would keep you from understanding them better this week?

Chapter 3

YOUR PURPOSE

*The power of a purpose lies not in its complexity
but in its simplicity. Say what you mean.*

C ulture born out of belief leads to transformation, innovation, and achievement. This is true no matter what the belief is, good or bad. To effectively create a culture that promotes alignment and benefits you, your people, and your company, that belief—or system of beliefs—must support a purpose.

People need to believe in and share a purpose—a destination they can rally around. Without a shared purpose, every new task, project, and crisis that comes up seems insurmountable because each person feels like they're on their own. You, as their leader, might feel this way too. Going it alone, day in and day out, leads to a feeling of loneliness in leadership.

It's scary in that place, dealing with everything on your own instead of as a team. Those on your team who aren't attached to a purpose will feel alienated from each other.

Your purpose identifies your destination and defines your journey: what you do every day and why you do it. Think of your destination as a flagged waypoint on a map. The flag—your banner—represents your purpose. No matter where anyone in your company is on the map, as long as they can see that banner, they'll be moving toward the same purpose.

YOUR PURPOSE IS YOUR BANNER

Think of your favorite sports team's banner, say, the Boston Red Sox. In *Game of Thrones*, each house has a distinct banner, and in Harry Potter, four banners distinguish each of the four houses at Hogwarts.

Now think about the people who identify with them. How important is each banner to the people they represent? Each group shares a purpose: to win the World Series, rule the seven kingdoms, or win the Quidditch match.

Can you imagine a Boston Red Sox fan not caring about winning the World Series? The banners represent people who *believe in their purpose wholeheartedly and without question.*

That's how important your purpose is. It's a banner that you and your people can rally around and enthusiastically support through transformation, innovation, and achievement.

Put your banner front and center in everything you do. Plant it firmly—a proud banner that everyone in your company can see and aim for, knowing that all they do aligns with that purpose.

Your Purpose Should Be Objective

A purpose can be either *subjective* or *objective*. To be successful, your purpose *must* be objective. Your people must have a clear understanding of the purpose and that's just not possible if it's subjective.

For example, if you state that your purpose is "to be a faith-based company," what does that mean to your people? *Faith-based* has many different connotations and people will perceive the term differently based on their own personal worldview. That's the problem with subjective purposes: Everyone interprets them a different way.

On the other hand, consider the purpose "feeding the homeless." It's clear, concise, and leaves no room for interpretation. Everyone knows what *feeding the homeless* means.

This clarity is critical, because people on your team must understand your purpose the way it is intended to be understood. They must comprehend its meaning with no ambiguity before they can commit to it.

Purpose and Alignment

When you buy into the purpose 100 percent, you create a structure and a path of alignment for your people. Every task, project, role, and goal align to that purpose and each person has the opportunity to align too. Working together with alignment like this leads to fulfillment for you and everyone involved.

Think about a time you did something really well at work that contributed to the company's purpose. You celebrated and everyone celebrated with you. Everyone shared your success.

Now think of a time you accomplished something at work that wasn't in line with the company's purpose. You probably felt different that time. People may have half-heartedly congratulated you, but that shared feeling of success just wasn't there. It was just you feeling sort of good about something but having no one to celebrate with and no one else to be happy for. There's a feeling of emptiness that accompanies success without shared purpose.

A shared purpose that people believe in is a powerful thing. People will put their personal wants and needs aside to support each other in their shared quest to support the purpose—to reach that destination. It offers them a way to serve something greater than themselves.

Define Your Purpose

Define your purpose with purpose. Yes, that sounds a bit redundant, but you really do have to be purposeful when you define your company's purpose. It isn't just something you make up on the fly. Put a lot of thought into it and make sure it says *exactly* what you want it to say. Define it with a carefully thought-out and properly constructed purpose.

A clear and concise purpose lets everyone know exactly where they're headed. It shows them the destination. Like any journey you go on, the more specific the destination, the easier it is for people to decide whether or not they want to come along. A clear purpose ensures you don't end up on a journey with people who would rather be somewhere else.

Your people and anyone who may be considering joining your team need to understand your purpose so they can make the right decision. Stay or leave. Accept a position or pass on it. Make that decision based on the clarity of the purpose and whether you can and should buy into it.

An ambiguous purpose doesn't give people enough information to make that decision. They may go along with it, but it doesn't mean anything to them, and they're not terribly committed to it. And we shouldn't be surprised by that. After all, you can't commit to something you don't believe in or don't understand. That only creates confusion and ambivalence.

> Your purpose becomes part of the definition of your company's culture. Together with guiding principles, it establishes the culture.

When your people can come to work every day knowing their role and how it aligns with the purpose of the company, they will feel differently. They will know their work *matters*. Every success will matter too, because it will be shared among everyone else who's working for the agreed upon purpose.

To identify your purpose, you have to ask yourself where you want to go. You need a destination. Once you have defined your company's purpose, write it down. Then figure out how to communicate it in a meaningful way to everyone on your team. You should then do the same for each department, team, and role.

Say that your destination as a company is to feed the homeless. That's a very clear purpose, but you have to make sure that anyone who works for you understands *the* purpose of their role—how *what they do* contributes to the big picture of feeding the homeless. To feed the homeless, you need a lot of things: money to buy the food, people to buy it, and people to prepare it.

This means breaking down your company's purpose into aligned purposes for each department, team, and individual. You might have a purpose for the team responsible for getting people to donate money for food, so they understand how they're contributing to the purpose. That way, any time they get a big donation, they can celebrate, and everyone else in the company can celebrate with them.

You need to define the purpose for teams and individuals whose contributions aren't so obviously aligned with the purpose. You might have people who keep the computers and networks running and the databases up to date so you can track all the donations, purchases, preparations, packages, and distributions. Without them, it wouldn't be possible for any of you to reach the company's destination or fulfill its purpose.

This is how you make sure everyone understands exactly how they contribute to the company's purpose. It's all very clear-cut and aligned, and there is zero ambiguity.

Beyond each team's purpose, you want to get even more granular and define the purpose of each project, role, and task. Wherever there is the possibility of misalignment or misunderstanding between what people do and how it contributes to the purpose, define it clearly.

Companies get caught up in high-level, convoluted (often pretentious) mission statements and statements of purpose that don't mean anything to anyone. They might look impressive, but if you need a dictionary or an encyclopedia to decipher their meaning, no one is likely to care about them or commit to them.

The power of a purpose lies not in its complexity but in its simplicity. It should be specific—not vague and never complicated. Think hard about your purpose, but don't think too hard about how you want to state it. Say what you mean.

Just like you would give someone clear directions to a precise location, your purpose needs to be as detailed as necessary to get them there but not too much detail that might cause confusion. You need to offer enough information for your people to decide whether or not they want to join you. Give them a clear picture of where you're headed, what's going to happen along the way, and, most importantly, *why*. When they read your purpose, they should be able to easily decide if they want to come along on your journey.

This purpose isn't something you create on your own and hand down to your employees. If you have a small company, invite everyone to participate in its construction. A company purpose for a larger company might be created by a high-level team, but when you get to the department and team level, include as many people from that department or team as you can. Through conversations with people, build a purpose that aligns with the company purpose. They need to come up with ideas that they own and will rally around. Giving your people a platform to share their ideas and involving them in the creation of the purpose gives them psychological ownership over their work. People will naturally own what they help to create.

You have a very specific role in this process. You are there to guide them and ensure the purpose aligns with the company purpose and fulfills the department's responsibility to that purpose. You are not there to micromanage or even offer ideas at first. If you get people in a room, tell them all your ideas, and then ask them to construct a purpose based on those ideas, you've immediately taken all the ownership away from them. **If *only your* ideas end up in the purpose, your people won't own them or buy into them.**

Don't come into the room with a preconceived idea of what you want the purpose to be. Here's why: People will sense that the meeting is a meaningless and manipulative formality to make them think they're creating the purpose when, in reality, you're just telling them what to do. Respect the fact that these are intelligent people with insight into your business that you may not have. If you let them speak, they will amaze you and maybe even surprise you. Give them that opportunity.

You are there to ensure alignment. If they end up with a purpose that misses the mark, you can step in by asking questions and allowing your people to arrive at conclusions for how to adjust the purpose on their own, but you should never, ever tell them what it's going to be.

Remember, the leader serves the purpose of the company and the people who work there. You have to be willing to go through a personal transformation to serve something bigger than yourself. This is the only way your people will feel like they're winning.

If you're used to making all the decisions and telling people what to do, this won't work. Instead, you are leveraging *all* that your people bring to the table—their hopes, preferences, traditions, experiences, and beliefs—to serve something greater than all of you. It's hard to fight that urge when you've been leading that way for a long time, but once you master the art of listening to your people—*really listening to them*—you'll begin to understand the value they possess, and you may wonder why you didn't do this sooner. You'll see how their ideas can build a purpose that reflects them and still aligns with the company purpose.

Your Purpose Will Evolve

Once you have the company, department, and individual purposes developed, you need to keep them in mind when you're recruiting new talent. Use them in your recruiting materials and in your interviews.

When someone new joins a team, you should address how their contributions align with the purpose. When I bring in a new person, I go to the team and say something like, "Hey folks, we've got a new team member. We've already established what our purpose is, but by bringing in a new team member, we need to ask ourselves: Is this still our purpose? Let's rebuild it with the new team member in mind." It may be that we end up in the same exact place, or it may be that we start over, but we re-establish our team's purpose based on a new member of our team and our culture. We calibrate and re-check our purpose as often as necessary to be sure that we are still aligned.

Include this person in the conversation. If you think back on when problems arise on teams, you might discover that many begin when you bring in new team members and assume that you can just tell them what the purpose is, rather than rebuilding the purpose *with* and *for* them. Remember, each new person has a unique worldview—hopes, preferences, traditions, experiences, and beliefs. They will affect the culture of the company and may affect the purpose. Take that into account with each new hire.

Take Kyle, for example. He brought in his own hopes, preferences, traditions, experiences, and beliefs, which all culminated in the passion to serve people so that everyone wins. Although he did not fully realize it at the time, his belief in the importance of supporting others influenced and expanded his team's purpose to include more opportunities to serve our clients and each other. His team could now do more to collectively support our company's purpose.

Revisiting the purpose will also make you aware of how the culture of the company is changing with each new person. This isn't a bad thing—don't look at it as a challenge to be overcome. Instead, embrace the diversity. Each person you add has the potential to broaden your company's understanding of the world and is key to preventing you from falling into the dreaded "this is how we've always done it" syndrome.

Companies like to say they're innovative, but if they are not open to expanding and evolving their culture, then how innovative are they? Take this as your opportunity to show how open you are to new worldviews. Welcome the person to your team and welcome them to the process of evolving its culture and redefining its purpose.

Test Your Purpose

You've created this purpose with your people in a way that's clear and concise. Everybody gets it, owns it, and wants to rally around it.

Next, you need to test it.

You do this by continuously questioning how each task aligns—or does not align—to the purpose. This is an ongoing process. You may discover your people are spending time on tasks that don't align and that need to go away, or you may find that the purpose needs to be adjusted to accommodate tasks necessary for the support of and alignment to the company purpose. Be open to changing the purpose when necessary. Again, this is not only an executive decision. Get your people in a room and talk about it. Evaluate it. Get their input, and once you have a consensus, rewrite the purpose. If the revision affects people's roles in a department or team, they may need to rewrite those purposes as well.

This may seem like a lot of work, but the conversation goes more quickly than you think. People care about what they do and how they contribute to a greater purpose, and they want to discuss this. Be patient and ensure everyone is involved in the process. With everyone's buy-in, they will approach their jobs with more energy and excitement, which will more than make up for any time you spent with them establishing purpose.

Chapter 3 Summary and Application

In aligning, the first step in pursuing employee fulfillment is to create a clearly defined culture. There is no room for confusion or uncertainty here. You need to give your people something definite to point toward if you truly want to serve them. You have to make sure everyone is aligned and onboard with where you are going—your purpose.

If purpose is *not* clearly defined, then your employees will feel unfulfilled. Without that connection to purpose, they'll think the tasks they do are meaningless. They'll get frustrated when their tasks don't align to your vision because you're both working under isolated purposes. This is why *everyone* throughout your entire organization must agree on your purpose. Remind yourself as often as necessary that the end goal is alignment, and you need to filter everything you do through it. Keep this in mind as you work to build your culture through purpose.

As you ponder this whole idea of purpose, ask yourself these questions:

1. What is your company's purpose?
   a. Is it objective?

    b. Has it been tested?

    c. Has the intent been communicated?

    d. Have you and everyone on the team aligned to it?

2. What about the company's purpose resonates with you the most?

3. What part of your belief system does it resonate with?

4. Choose someone on your team this week to share with how your belief system connects with your company's purpose.

Chapter 4

YOUR GUIDING PRINCIPLES

Guiding principles guide our behavior.
They give us permission to hold each other
accountable to the way we treat each other
on the journey to accomplishing our purpose.

C ulture born out of belief—belief in a purpose—is essential. Our actions as we support that purpose are governed by our *guiding principles*, which are the other side of culture.

Guiding principles guide our behavior. They give us permission to hold ourselves and each other accountable to the way we treat each other on the journey to accomplishing our purpose. Your culture needs to be born out of belief, but not just any belief system, belief in an agreed upon purpose and belief in a set of principles. Your company may refer to guiding principles as *core values* and that's fine—either term works. The important thing here is that you have something.

Just as a thoroughly developed purpose shapes your culture, identifying your guiding principles completes it. The full picture of your culture is incomplete without them. Your people need these principles so they can clearly see how they should interact with one another on a daily basis.

Every culture has these values. My family's values have guided my children's behavior since they were very young. If we were going camping, they understood the purpose of the trip (to go camping) and could prepare for it. They also knew how they were expected to behave on the long drive to the campground. If they abandoned our family values and fought, screamed, and whined at each other the whole way to the campground, then no one would want to go camping. We would end up at our destination, but we'd get there pretty disgusted with each other. This isn't the culture I wanted for my family, and it's not the culture you want for your company.

Everybody wins where there is clarity and transparency.

Define Your Guiding Principles

Guiding principles are critical to both you and your

people in achieving the purpose of your company, team, and individual roles. Remember, the purpose is our compass and shows us *where* we are going, but the guiding principles show us *how* to get there. In an effort to align, one cannot operate without the other. Success depends on the two working in mutual harmony.

Consider a body of water with the purpose of becoming drinking water. The water is carefully curated, cleaned, and purified before being sent off for consumption. We have to be cautious about what goes into the water and make sure that what comes out is safe enough to drink. We can't just take polluted water, add it to our drinking water, and expect it to achieve the purpose of being consumable. Likewise, we wouldn't expect a swimming pool or a pond used for fishing to meet the same standards as water from which we're drinking.

When you take the time to clearly define the guiding principles with your people, you establish expectations and set a standard for anyone new to your body of water—your culture. The guiding principles help everyone understand the necessary elements in how your purpose is accomplished. Without clear and consistent guiding principles, you unintentionally set your people up to fail. They may know their purpose, but they are lost without a unified idea of how to get there.

One of our company's guiding principles is to communicate with integrity. This principle allows people to have an expectation when they talk to another person. Each person expects the other person to converse with integrity.

This sounds like an obvious and easy expectation because most people will tell you they already communicate with integrity. But issues arise because people have different definitions of integrity based on their experience with the word and the concept. You could have someone on a team who thinks communicating with integrity means saying things that you wish were true, while another believes it means saying things you know are true. There's a big difference between those definitions—it can mean the difference between people telling you what you want to hear instead of what you need to hear.

Just as you had conversations with your people about the company's purpose and how everything each department, team, and individual does aligns with the agreed upon purpose, you have to have conversations about principles too. Remember that alignment requires full comprehension and full commitment. You have to build your guiding principles with your team and employees for people to understand them and commit to them. You can't decide this for your people and then just present it to them. They need to have skin in the game. Working with them will ensure buy-in.

When you fail to define your guiding principles to every person in your company, you're leaving the culture up to interpretation. If you claim to truly care about culture, you will spend the time to get this right. Your people must own these principles like they own their purpose and their culture, and they have to live by them.

Defining your guiding principles prevents any issues with leaders talking to their employees about behaviors that fall outside of these principles. For example, you might be annoyed by a certain personality type, but with the guiding principles in place, you can't reprimand an employee for personality quirks just because you may find them annoying. You can't be subjective about what's okay and what's not okay. As long as their behavior aligns with the principles, you can't take it upon yourself to "correct" them.

A classic example from my workplace is the guiding principle of serving people and honoring everybody on your team. You honor their role and responsibilities. So, if you owe someone on your team a report by 8:30 and you're running late, it's okay to shoot them a text saying, "Hey, I know I owe you that report at 8:30. I had to drop my daughter off at school. I'll be in at 8:15 but won't be able to get that report to you until 8:45." A person who sends this text has lived up to our definition of the guiding principle of serving people, so no one should be jumping all over them for showing up fifteen minutes late. The person honored the role and responsibilities of the other person and met our expectations of what we believe serving people means. If we had a principle stating "everyone should absolutely be on time for work every day no matter what" then you might have to have a conversation with the person, but that's not a sensible principle for most businesses.

Guiding principles set clear expectations around behavior and culture. Without them, people aren't sure how they're supposed to behave. Without clear expectations, they have nothing to shoot for, no way to succeed, and cannot feel fulfilled.

Guiding Principles and Alignment

Your company's culture is comprised of the belief systems around your purpose and your guiding principles. When you define your purpose and your principles, you've defined your culture. When you define your culture, you have the opportunity for alignment. If you don't define your culture, alignment falls flat.

Comprehending and committing to the culture must happen to create and maintain alignment. The purpose and principles at the foundation of your culture are standard and a litmus test for gauging behaviors, actions, and how people spend their time at work. With these things in place, you don't have to worry about being subjective in explaining your expectations to your people of correcting behavior. There is no ambiguity because they helped you build these ideals, and they committed to them.

If someone lies to you or doesn't tell you the whole truth, you can say to them, "You know that communicating with integrity is part of our culture. You know what it means because we discussed it, and you committed to it."

Compare this to, "Hey man, I feel like you lied to me," which makes it about the individual's actions, while the former comment is about a commitment two people made to one another. A statement like, "I don't like to be lied to," or "I don't feel like you're telling me the whole story" feels very different from a reminder of the commitment to communicate with integrity. When you make it about how the person's actions affected you, you open a door for the employees to take. Making it about a commitment they made gives them a chance to re-commit.

Your culture should be a win-win-win for you, your people, and your company. To make this possible, you have to eliminate ambiguity, unclear or changing expectations, and personal vendettas—or anything that can be perceived as personal vendettas. The goal is to create alignment and adhere to that alignment. It's up to you as the leader to set the example for everyone else. This is how you set your people up for winning.

Think about that for a moment. When there is alignment, everyone knows the purpose, their place in it, and how to get there. Does it get any better than that as a leader? When that happens, a switch goes on and your job changes because your people are aware, and they are actively taking ownership for your organization. In a way, it becomes self-sustaining. Instead of wearing yourself out managing people, they manage themselves and their work—now you get to lead.

Write Your Guiding Principles

While the purpose of your company is developed through input from your employees and shaped to satisfy the purpose of the company by the leader, you may want to take a slightly more formal approach with writing your guiding principles. This gives your people a starting point for understanding your expectations around their behavior.

I begin with the most basic principles that define who I am and what I expect from people with whom I interact. Like communicating with integrity, for example. I would not want anyone working with me or for me who doesn't value telling the truth, or who doesn't think they'd be able to adhere to this principle.

Beyond this principle, I have a list that defines my idea of the perfect coworker or employee. When I began working on this list, I thought about the people I liked working with and I also thought about the people I spent the most time with on behavioral issues. What was the first group of people doing that made them easier to work with? What was so troublesome about the other group?

These values have to relate to the purpose. They can't simply be reactions to my own personal pet peeves. Remember, once you define the purpose and the principles, you make them the boss. Everything you do should align with the culture and support the purpose, including your guiding principles.

Think about it like this: You and your team have taken the time and put thought into creating the perfect boss. You've discussed and written down the description of this boss. Your boss defines what you do at work and why, and now it's up to that boss to show you how to show up, behave, and treat each other.

OUR GUIDING PRINCIPLES

When we wrote our guiding principles, I started with those that were most important to me and shared them with my people. We discussed them, revised them, and added to them, then we wrote them in a way that was crystal clear to everyone.

- Choose a Positive Mindset
- Aspire to Lead
- Communicate with Integrity
- Learn with Humility
- Pursue Profit
- Establish Trust
- Serve People
- Readily Adapt
- Celebrate Innovation
- Delight Clients
- Overcome Fear

As with purpose, there needs to be 100 percent clarity around your guiding principles, so you need to discuss them with your people to ensure you all have the same understanding of their meaning.

If your boss—the guiding principles—isn't working out for some reason, have a conversation about it. Just as you can revise the purpose of your company, department, team, and role, you can also revise the guiding principles. Expect this to happen as people evolve, join, or leave your team and as your purpose and priorities change.

Discussing, defining, and writing your guiding principles, making them the boss, and being open to changing them allows you, as the leader, to offer clear expectations to your people that they own, believe in, and will rally around.

Embrace Employee Diversity

Diversity is another one of those buzzwords that's typically defined within a narrow and limited scope. Employee diversity refers to the uniqueness in the differences that make us who we are based on each person's worldview. Embracing your people's diversity means not just being aware of, but deeply _understanding_ how that contributes to your purpose and principles—your culture.

Embracing employees' diversity isn't limited to your existing team. Just like your company's purpose, the company's guiding principles and their meaning must be communicated to anyone new you bring in. A candidate should be made aware of them before being hired to ensure you aren't bringing in a person whose own values will conflict with those of the company.

During orientation at my company, we spend time talking about our guiding principles in a way that's less informative and more constructive. I'll explain communicating with integrity to new recruits and then ask, "What do you guys think about that? Are there aspects of this guiding principle that we could make clearer?" I have a conversation with them around that guiding principle and I get to know how they see themselves aligning or not aligning with it. I want to know if it means something different to them, or if it needs to be stated with more clarity. Discussions like this with people allow you to rewrite and refine your guiding principles in a way that creates greater definition for your people.

These conversations are so important, yet often overlooked by leaders. Think about it, though. You've spent a bunch of money and resources finding and attracting the right new person to your company, and you're about to spend more time and money training and onboarding them so that they can contribute. You obviously saw something in this person that your company needs—that's why you hired them in the first place. They have tremendous value, and you owe it to them, to yourself, and to your company to welcome them into the conversation and share their value.

Think about how this person feels when you're asking for their input on the very first day. They will feel empowered knowing their voice matters in defining the culture of your company. They will leave work that day feeling like they already belong—like this is *their company*.

Instead of asking them to put aside all their hopes, preferences, traditions, experiences, and beliefs so they can automatically adopt this new culture, you are embracing their diversity and looking for ways that it can benefit your company. You're welcoming them as an integral part of your culture right from the start, and it's the first step in understanding how that diversity contributes to culture.

Their Innovation is Your Transformation

This is part of your transformation too. You are becoming a person who's comfortable transferring ownership of your company's culture (purpose and principles) from your position of authority to the shared culture of your employees. Together, you define the culture and then you make that culture the boss.

Leaders often feel threatened by their employees' hopes, preferences, traditions, experiences, and beliefs. Don't be threatened—flip it around and see the value. Respect these things. Let your people know that you're interested in what they have to bring to the table and that they matter.

As you interact with people this way, you'll begin to evolve your leadership skills. It will change how you feel about your people and yourself. It will change the way people see you, too. By putting yourself aside and focusing on all that your people have to offer, they will see you as a leader who values them, and they'll be more engaged in their work.

Conversations with your people to define culture (purpose and principles) is how you practice your leadership and also how you provide professional development to your people. As you transform, so do they.

Chapter 4 Summary and Application

Culture needs to be established from belief in a purpose and guiding principles. Guiding principles help to do just that—guide. These principles inform our behavior and allow us to hold each other accountable in how we treat each other as we work toward purpose. Guiding principles are necessary to tell your people how to get to the goal.

Again, clarity is critical here. You're setting up how you want your people to achieve their purpose; you can't leave them wondering about what you mean. The ultimate goal is to create alignment, and without clear guiding principles, people have different expectations (often unspoken) about behavior, which only leads to frustration. Frustration, in turn, eventually leads to being unfulfilled.

Once you've written your guiding principles in a way that people can comprehend and commit to, you've finished defining your culture. You began defining it with purpose and now, combined with guiding principles, it's complete. Remember that it's not about demanding behavior today; you and your people are just committing to head in that direction. By doing this, you have now put your banner up. With purpose, you've set the destination, and with guiding principles, you know how you're going to get there.

At this point, review your guiding principles to ensure nothing has been left out. Remember, you're making these things the boss, so you cannot expect people to adhere to something that hasn't been discussed with them. They need to see and understand the boss if you expect them to follow it. You might struggle to hand off the "boss" title to your culture. But true transformation moves you away from traditional management to leadership based in alignment.

1. List your company's guiding principles.
2. Choose one of your company's guiding principles and write down what you think it looks like to live it out. What are some specific scenarios where you could apply it?
3. After doing this, choose three people this week within your sphere of influence. Ask them what they

think it would look like to live out that same guiding principle. Now, compare the results.

4. Based on the results, how effective is the current definition of that guiding principle? Does it provide enough clarity for people to comprehend and commit to it?

Chapter 5

CULTIVATE CULTURE

Tying purpose to culture takes momentum, and the moment you miss out on an opportunity to reinforce why your people are accomplishing a task or working on a project, you lose momentum in the shift of culture.

At this point, you've defined the sum of the hopes, preferences, traditions, experiences, and beliefs of the people in your company. You understand the *current* culture.

You have also determined the purpose and principles you and your people believe in and can all rally around. You have a destination and a pathway to get there. Cultivating your culture is the selfless act of continuously and consistently asking: How does this project, task, service, or product drive our purpose? Think of your purpose and guiding principles as a roadmap for charting the culture you're going to cultivate.

Shifting from one culture to another is a continuous process. Just like steering a boat on the ocean, you'll head in one direction and the wind, waves, and weather will push you in another, and you'll have to readjust your course. This can happen internally whenever something in your company changes, such as adding a new team member. External forces, such as changes in your industry, also affect your course and, again, you'll need to readjust every time this happens. Can you recall a time when a change in your personnel, company goals, or outside forces made you rethink your company culture?

This is why having a purpose is so critical to your culture. Regardless of which way the wind blows, that purpose—your *banner*—shows you which way to go while your guiding principles show you how to get there.

Shifting culture in your company requires clarity. *You* know your purpose and your principles. Now it's up to you to clearly communicate them to your people.

Make Culture the Boss

Your purpose statement won't provide enough clarity to cultivate your culture. You have to make culture *the boss* and pay close attention when it "speaks."

Culture needs to be the decision maker. It needs to determine what you *do*—the projects you work on, tasks you accomplish, services you provide, and products you create. Your company's culture drives the actions of the business, your department, team, and each person's role. Until you start making those decisions based on your purpose, you cannot shift the culture.

There can be no ambiguity when it comes to culture, which is why *it*—and not *you*—has to be in charge. If there's any uncertainty around your company's purpose, your people will never be onboard.

Consider a scenario where one of your employees is assigned a task and they ask, "Why am I doing this?" As long as that task serves the purpose, you can point to your purpose and say, "Because this is our purpose and doing this task is how you serve our purpose today." Doing it this way makes for an easy explanation that gives clear direction and allows the person to see, without any ambiguity, how they're contributing. It also eliminates the tasks, projects, services, and products that do *not* serve the purpose.

You must connect *every* task back to the purpose consistently. Even if you think you've already explained the connection to your people, you must repeat it every time you talk about a task or a project. Tie it back to the purpose of the company, the department, and the role. Tying purpose to culture takes momentum, and the moment you miss out on an opportunity to reinforce why your people are accomplishing a task or working on a project, you lose momentum in the shift of culture.

Consistency in explaining the *why* makes it clear that the purpose statement you've created for the company, the department, and the role makes the decisions for the organization, not you as the leader.

Defend Culture with Leadership

Once you've defined your culture (purpose and principles), it's all about consistency. As the leader, you do this by being consistent in how you lead.

First, you have to make sure that every task you assign is tied back to purpose. Assigning a person to a project or job that doesn't align with the purpose is confusing and isn't fair to the employee. It will leave them feeling unfulfilled—like they're not winning.

You must also be consistent with adherence to principles. You and your people have to align with the guiding principles you've defined, and when someone behaves outside these principles, you must address the elephant in the room. You do this with conversations, and those conversations might be uncomfortable at times, but you absolutely have to have them. Remember, you've all agreed to be held accountable to these guiding principles. So, these conversations are just a reminder of your commitment—not behavioral management. If you allow things to just slide, you're basically condoning behavior that's out of line with the culture. This tells your people that you don't take it seriously. What kind of message does that send to them and how would you expect them to react? You're supposed to be the role model and the defender of culture and your people look to you to set the standard.

Again, this is *simple, not easy*. Expect to have some tough conversations. It's hard at first, but believe me, it will become *so much easier* the more you practice it. The payoffs will make it all worth it.

Shift the Culture

By writing your purpose and your principles, you've outlined the destination of where you want your culture to be. It's based on beliefs in your purpose and principles. You also know where you are now, and you can begin shifting from your current position to that new one.

This process of shifting the culture is one of clarity—providing clarity to your people. One purpose statement may not provide enough clarity for everyone in the organization to shift their culture. If there is any ambiguity, you won't be able to shift culture. What if you assign a particular task to an employee and their question to you—either spoken or unspoken—is: *Why do I have to do this?* It can't be "because I said so." Your solution cannot be to impose your authority because that leads to compliance or defiance.

Instead, answer the question. Here's how I would answer it: "Well, here's the company's purpose. Here's your department's purpose, which aligns with the company's purpose, and here is the purpose of your role, which aligns with your team's, your department's, and the company's purpose. Does that make sense?"

Don't be surprised if an employee asks that question and you don't have an answer for them. In this process, you will discover tasks that don't align with your purpose, and you'll need to consider whether you should be doing them. You may also discover tasks that need to be done and maybe the purpose needs to be adjusted. Culture is not just a destination—it's a journey. There will be changes, but each change will bring you closer to that ideal culture for you, your people, and your company at that time.

Be Responsible to Your Purpose

To cultivate the culture, you will need to be responsible to your purpose, as opposed to being the authority in the room. I don't need to direct an employee to accomplish a task if they understand their role involves a responsibility to that task because of its relationship to the purpose.

This is your job every day as the leader. You're not there to tell people what to do but to connect the dots between what you and your people are doing and why you're doing it.

If you go through this process and you still feel like your primary job is to make sure all the tasks and projects get done, then you need to continue to align your team. That's not how you should be spending your time—it's not even really your responsibility anymore. Your job is to create alignment between tasks and purpose.

When you make the conversation about authority, then you communicate very clearly that you only care about what the person can do for you. You show that you don't care about cultivating the culture. You don't care about who the person is or who you want to help them become. When you communicate that message through authority, you eliminate any chance of the employees finding fulfillment in their work. They'll still do their tasks and projects, but they won't be truly fulfilled in what they're doing, and the results will not be as good for them or the company.

I say this to my people, "I'm the owner, but I'm not the boss. The boss is our purpose and it dictates what we do." You can say the same thing to your people: "I'm the owner, president, CEO, manager, team lead, whatever—but the purpose is in charge."

If you don't make the effort to make these connections between work and purpose, you'll be operating on a lot of assumptions. This is where shortcuts are likely to get made and shortcuts are devastating. You're assuming the tasks and projects your people are currently working on are what they should be doing. This might happen because people have been doing them since you started the job or the business. Maybe you just inherited these tasks from another leader, or you had to do them at first and your people have kept doing them out of habit, even though they no longer serve the purpose. No one investigated whether they still align to your purpose.

Leaders also tend to make assumptions that if somebody's asking a question, they don't know how to accomplish a task or work on a project or they're trying to get out of doing it. The reality is, they might literally *just want to know* because they believe so deeply in the purpose and want to be aligned with it. It's up to you to help them connect the dots so they can feel like they're winning.

When people ask why, they're typically seeking fulfillment. Believe the best about them.

Commit to Your Principles

Many companies post their guiding principles or core values on the website, but then there are the unspoken principles or values that reside within each leader. Because of these varying values, employees have to behave a certain way when they're dealing with one leader than they do when they're dealing with another. That's confusing.

If you're cultivating your organizational culture toward a belief in a set of principles, then those principles cannot change from leader to leader. There *must* be consistency. Your ability to shift principles—and as a result, culture—from where it is now to where you want it to be relies on your employees understanding how to interact with each other at work.

You have developed a set of principles based on the perfect coworker or employee, and everyone agreed, "I absolutely agree with this. I believe in it. If everyone at work had these principles, I would love coming to work with them every day." Now you can coach people toward those principles. You don't want to manage behaviors; you want to *coach* them. This is an essential part of alignment: coaching behaviors to align with mutually agreed upon principles.

If you are joining a company that already has principles in place, it's up to you to learn them and understand what they mean in the context of the company. As a leader, you will need to be able to communicate them to your employees.

Misunderstanding or a misalignment around principles can create the largest culture gap for employees. For example, if you have a guiding principle that says people have to establish trust, no one will disagree with that statement. Most people understand that you need to have trust in a workplace. But if the leader's *interpretation* of establishing trust is, "My employees need to earn my trust," yet the *intended meaning* is that there's personal responsibility to establish trust, then, not surprisingly, misalignment happens.

Leaders must comprehend and commit to the principles, they must understand their meaning as they were written, and they must be able to communicate them clearly to their people. If one of my people isn't communicating with integrity, I have to be willing to have a conversation with them about it. I also need to be able to remind them what that principle actually means and what they said or did that didn't align with it.

Whenever I have a conversation with people with the goal of helping them realign with our culture, I ask myself some questions after our talk. Try these out yourself and see what kind of answers you get:

- Did my conversation with them fuel them or deplete them?
- Did this get them excited about this principle and living it out or did this demoralize them?
- Did I move them toward their commitment or away from it?

I know from experience how to end up with the wrong outcome in these discussions. If you say something like, "The way you didn't communicate with integrity upset me," now you're making it personal and you're demoralizing the person. When you do this, the person will respond by moving away from you and away from their commitment.

You *have to* extract yourself, as the leader, from the equation. This can be hard for leaders if you're feeling prideful, hurt, annoyed, or disappointed. You can't be part of it. If you make yourself part of it, you're essentially making yourself the *boss* again, rather than the *leader*. Focus on serving *them*. If I act offended by an employee, then that becomes part of the conversation. But if I can remain an objective third party and guide them to a fuller understanding of where they fell short of that guiding principle, they can accept it. I do this by first sitting with an employee to understand their perception of the incident. Then, based on what they communicate, I identify any deficits in the way they acted and how they may not be living up to the fullness of the guiding principle. Finally, we discuss how to get back on track and make plans to move forward in their commitment to that guiding principle. It's absolutely vital that you ensure their understanding of the big picture and how to continue in their dedication to your guiding principles and, thus, your culture. Stay present in the conversation until alignment is gained.

People will appreciate your candor and transparency and many times they'll even thank you for pointing it out to them. They want to align—they want to be part of the team. They want to know their contributions support the purpose. Help them. They'll be glad you did.

Alignment between Words and Actions

Sometimes leaders can be doing a phenomenal job communicating guiding principles to their people and holding them accountable. However, they don't always hold themselves accountable. In other words, they say one thing, but act a different way. This won't fly for your employees and they will notice it immediately. Again, you're the role model—what you say and do sets the standard for everyone else.

You might also see this in your employees. You work with them to understand the principles and they tell you they get it and they're committed to the culture, yet their behaviors tell a very different story. When you see this happening, you have to act. Think about whether this person really is a good fit for your organization.

This can be especially difficult to deal with when you have a high achiever on your team who thinks they can get away with treating others badly. You don't want to get rid of the person, but if they're unwilling to change and commit to the principles you have all agreed to, you must act. Letting them get away with that behavior communicates to everyone else that achievement is the boss and culture (purpose and principles) takes a back seat. It's a great way to lose good people who are committed to the culture if that's your goal.

Tolerating bad behavior is a mistake every time. Tolerating people who say that they want to commit to the company's guiding principles yet live out a very different version of these principles each and every day prevents fulfillment for every employee who witnesses the behavior. There needs to be a strong connection between people and the culture, and when culture is a moving target based on who the leader is or how well one of their teammates achieves, your people will be disillusioned. They'll stay and exhibit bad behavior too, or they'll choose to leave.

Did I Mention This is Hard?

Consistency in how you communicate principles, how you act them out, and how you hold people accountable to them will eventually shift your culture to where you want it to be. While this is happening, even during the most difficult aspects of it, you will begin to see a difference in your people and in yourself. The stress will decrease. People won't see you as some kind of taskmaster, but as someone who's on their side, wanting them to join you in shared success.

They will feel known, heard, and valued. They'll know you're for *them*—not for your own personal agenda or an unspoken company agenda. Everything is on the table and there is no ambiguity or uncertainty.

This is hard. It really is. I know I'm making it sound simple, but when you put it into action, you'll realize how difficult it can be to get it right every single time for every single person every single day.

Like all difficult things, you need a big reason to commit to it. You can't just be driving alignment for yourself or your company. You can't be doing it with the hopes of a big promotion or a raise. You need something bigger than that to drive you.

For me, **the foundation of leadership is loving and serving people toward their fulfillment**. *Hopefully*, it's the same for you. Caring about others will propel you through the difficult process of cultivating culture. Remember that you are doing this to serve people who have come to your company and are looking to you for leadership. You are responsible for their success. If you think you're only responsible for the success of a department, or a project, or a task, then the hardship of cultivating culture will not be worth it.

It won't motivate you to push through the difficulties, and you will always take the path of least resistance.

I want you to really see your team and remind yourself that you have it within you to make it possible for them to be fulfilled at work. That is an awesome responsibility, and you can do it. As you keep doing it, you'll hear from them. They'll communicate to you how they feel known, heard, and valued, and that their work matters. They'll communicate it to you nonverbally too with the commitment, dedication, and passion they bring to their roles. These changes will produce amazing results that would not be possible if you had forgone alignment and adopted a taskmaster or behavioral management leadership style.

Chapter 5 Summary and Application

Hopefully this chapter showed you again why I say that alignment is *simple, not easy*. Cultivating your culture is a continuous and never-ending process, but you're not starting from scratch—your company has a culture and, through conversation with your people, you have defined the culture you want to have. Cultivating culture is hard work, but if you truly love people and want the best for them, you will find the motivation you need to keep cultivating the culture that allows your people to be fulfilled. They will feel like they're winning every morning they step foot in your office and every evening when they say goodbye.

I can tell you from firsthand experience that, at some point, you *will* want to give up or give in. There will be days when you want to simply tell people what to do. You'll want to skip those important conversations and just do whatever it takes to make sure tasks are done and projects are completed. Fight that urge. Expect and embrace the challenge. Remind yourself that you are better than that. You're not a taskmaster—you're a leader who has more to offer than just making sure things get done. You can offer professional development to your people through your leadership. You can change their lives for the better by the way you choose to lead.

Take every opportunity to shift your culture toward the culture you believe it should be, even when it's difficult. *Especially* when it's difficult. Make that culture the boss and be open to changing it as your purpose and guiding principles change. It's a constant evolution. As you begin to see results, communicate with your leadership and try to get them onboard with cultivating culture throughout the company.

1. Have you taken the time to identify your culture?
    a. Do you understand the worldview of everyone on your team?
    b. How would you summarize the combination of those worldviews?

    c. What are some potential points of conflict within your team based on the worldviews?

    d. How would someone from outside your organization summarize the combination of those worldviews?

2. Are there changes needed with the company's purpose or guiding principles?

3. What will you do this week to begin shifting or cultivating the culture (purpose and principles)?

4. What will you stop doing this week to cultivate the culture (purpose and principles)?

KYLE'S STORY: PART ONE

Kyle's excitement to enter a field of work that he witnessed his father find so much fulfillment in soon vanished. He felt like he was wasting his time trying to please everyone's individual passion instead of a single, organizational purpose. He never found a way to win. At the end of each day, Kyle grew increasingly disheartened, burnt out, and alone.

Kyle wasn't even sure what he was looking for, but he was equipped with established hopes, preferences, traditions, experiences, and beliefs from his upbringing that he craved in all areas of his life. Kyle knew that he somehow wanted to be involved in creating and cultivating culture, although he didn't know how to define that for himself at the time. Even without the precise words to express himself, his résumé objective stated in so many words that he was looking to be a part of creating culture wherever he was and in whatever capacity that he was needed. This was what caught my eye when his résumé came across my desk.

In Kyle's interview, I spent a lot of time defining our culture. I talked to him about our purpose and our guiding principles in a way that connects to our beliefs. Through our conversation,

I was able to identify that he is someone whose worldview would add value to the culture I wanted to cultivate.

During Kyle's onboarding, I had a chance to meet with him and the new hires in an informal setting. Once people have been exposed to our culture, I like the opportunity to check in and make sure they remember why we hired them in the first place—that they are valuable for who they are. I told Kyle that I saw a kindness in him, an ability to learn with humility, and that he was a lifelong learner. I never once fixated on what he could do for me or my company, but on what he was already contributing to our culture, just by being himself.

Kyle later told me that this small interaction had changed his life. He'd always prided himself on those traits as unique to him, but never thought that they could be seen as valuable outside of his personal life. This narrative that his worldview—hopes, preferences, traditions, experiences, and beliefs—could never lead to fulfillment at work were immediately shattered. For the first time, he was able to see that fulfillment at work was possible and it gave him a thirst for more.

CULTURE MAP

Think of it as a treasure map, in order to reach the treasure (your destination or purpose) the map must identify where the treasure is. However, without defining where you are starting from you will have no idea how to get there. The definition of your current culture is the sum of the worldviews of you and everyone on your team. Take the time to truly understand everyone's worldview:

- Hopes
- Preferences
- Traditions
- Experiences
- Beliefs

Connect with Alignment Leadership at book.alignleadthrive.com/align to access resources that help you build your unique culture map.

Step Two

CREATE PRIORITIES

Prioritizing time is the ability to understand how all tasks connect back to purpose. Prioritizing tasks will lead to transformation, innovation, and achievement for your employees.

Chapter 6

PREPARE TO GET PRACTICAL

*Use your purpose to establish
what you're going to do next.*

Time is the most precious commodity that we have at our disposal, and we are given complete freedom in how we use it. I'll give you an illustration. Let's say I have a full jar of marbles. Each marble in this jar represents every Saturday that exists for a child between the ages of zero and eighteen—936 marbles—a lot of marbles. One marble. One Saturday. When you look at one marble, you can see the value of that one Saturday, but all together in the jar, they tend to lose their value. Seeing so many marbles makes you think you will never run out. Fast-forward, all four of my kids are now older than eighteen. In a blink, all my Saturdays with my kids are gone—empty jar. What did I do with them? I can tell you right now, I didn't value every single one of them. As the jar emptied, each marble became very precious; we could see the end coming and regret started to settle in.

The value of time is something you control; nobody controls that for you. Why is that so important as it relates to alignment or this concept of fulfillment? Because if we don't understand how to prioritize our time, we never understand how to value it. I value those Saturdays more now than I did when I was raising my kids. That is called regret—the feeling that I should have done more with the time. I had it in my hands, I controlled it, and I could have done more. This preciousness of time and this concept of fulfillment collide at work and at home in how we prioritize our time.

How do you prioritize time if you've got one hundred things that you could be doing? The way you do that is through purpose. After all the work that we've done to cultivate culture, we now get to test it, refine it, change it, adapt. This is now the chance that we get to understand if we created a purpose that can be the guide for how we prioritize our time. And if it doesn't inform us on how to prioritize every task, every project, every conversation, every email, then we must go back to purpose and force it to be our teacher.

We must have a purpose that can be comprehended in a way that allows us to understand what to do **next**. What is the most important thing you can do today? The answer is the **next** thing. When you prioritize your time through the lens of purpose, it gives you a chance, just a chance, to move closer to the destination. We look at where we're going—we look at that purpose—and we make a determination. What do we think we should do next to get there? And then we do that thing. We refine it. We change it. We learn from it.

The world teaches us that accomplishment and achievement is getting as many things done as we possibly can. That's just not true, not if we're going to serve a purpose—a destination. We don't want to be mice on a wheel just spinning. We're literally going nowhere. And yet we do that because we don't prioritize our time. We don't let purpose dictate what we do next. If you don't prioritize, you're not valuing time. I'm telling you that there will be regret. And if there's regret, there can't be fulfillment.

The number one reason why a lot of anxiety exists for employees is because they put their heart and soul into what they're doing. Yet they don't know if it's what they should be doing or when they should be doing it. Purpose allows us to take advantage of, to control, to be the pilot of how we spend our time. You must fight to prioritize your time, because wasting time feels terrible. And it's not just at work—it's everywhere. But if we can connect what we're doing and why to this purpose, this thing that we've already connected to with our beliefs, we can actually feel like we are redeeming the time.

You've put a lot of work into step one. You have a better understanding of what culture is, and you know that to create a culture that sparks transformation, innovation, and achievement, it has to be based on a belief in your purpose and principles.

I have been down this road you're traveling right now, and if you're doing the work consistently, then I think I can make an observation about your organization and your people. As you're communicating the purpose and guiding principles of the company to everyone in a way that they comprehend and commit to, then you're cultivating culture daily and you're seeing a change in your people and the culture they share. You're even feeling differently about yourself as a leader.

Now it's time to leverage what you've accomplished. With culture as boss, it's time to look to your purpose to discover the work ahead. Where do you start? Under traditional management, you might look to what you've always done first. That's not how it works when purpose is our guide. With traditional management, you might look at what's most urgent. Again—not so when aligning.

This is the opposite of what you've always done because now you have a defined purpose to align with, and that's going to require a different approach. The first action you will take here in step two is to use your purpose to establish what you're going to do next.

Don't be daunted. You can do this. If you feel over-whelmed, remind yourself *why* you're doing this. You've got the hardest part behind you—identifying the culture. Those same people who benefited from that effort are still here and they can continue to benefit from your leadership if you're willing to stay committed to them. You can do this for them by showing them what to do for the company and everyone in the company to accomplish their purpose. You're not here to order people around and make sure everything gets done—you're here to connect the dots for them between what they do and the purpose of their role, team, and company.

This chapter will prepare you to meet with your people to prioritize everyone's time. I'll break down all the steps required to ensure that when you show up, you're ready to serve them well.

Connect Priorities with Purpose

Using purpose as your destination is like setting your GPS and heading for the coordinates instead of wandering aimlessly, hoping you'll arrive at your destination. With everyone heading in the same direction, you'll see stress reduce and the opportunity for fulfillment will come alive. The tasks they have to complete to get to that destination are like waypoints along their path with each one getting them closer and closer to satisfying their purpose.

Compare this with simply handing each person a map and telling them to meet somewhere. No one knows where they're going, how to get there, or when to arrive. You might know, but without giving them a clear direction, they have no idea. You can laugh, but I've seen this happen many times in the workplace. The leader assumes everyone knows where they're going and how to get there, then the leader is stunned when everyone heads off in a different direction and arrives there in different ways and at different times.

If you want to create a lot of stress for your people, don't give them the next waypoint. Don't tell them what they need to be doing right now to successfully get to their destination on time; instead, wait until after they've accomplished the wrong task at the wrong time—that's not fulfilling to anyone.

This seems cruel, doesn't it? Yet that scenario plays out daily in many organizations. It's not surprising that so few people love their workplace and what they do there. Don't let that happen. Take the time to understand how the tasks your people do and the deadlines that drive them align with the company's purpose.

Be clear on this. Write it down. Make a chart, a list, or a timeline. Before you meet with your people to explain what they're going to do and when they're going to do it, ensure you understand and can explain it in a way that makes how they're aligned with the purpose obvious.

Remember again why you're doing this—you love these people and want to serve them toward fulfillment. You don't want them to feel stressed or burned out. They need clarity; they need alignment.

This is true leadership. Do this right and you will achieve the fulfillment as a leader that you've been seeking, and your people will achieve the fulfillment they need in their roles. If you need help or more explanation, review step one, continue to cultivate your culture, and visit alignleadthrive.com for online resources. Humble yourself—ask for help. I have been where you are, and I have relied on my community of great leaders to help me evolve as a leader—none of us gets there alone.

Stress Versus Healthy Tension

Leveraging purpose to identify the work that needs to be done will set the stage for a conversation free from stress. You'll be able to talk to your people about the time they spend on the tasks they do and how they align with the purpose you've established.

This doesn't mean you will have your feet up on the desk, twiddling your thumbs when you have the conversation. You won't be sitting cross-legged on the floor holding hands and singing Kumbaya either. In fact, expect some tension.

You have a huge project with a deadline that will be difficult to meet. Healthy tension will exist when you connect that project to your company's purpose in a way that identifies how this will be a win for everyone. There will be excitement and an eagerness to jump in and get started. Instead of the *hopelessness* that accompanies stress, there will be an overwhelming feeling of *hopefulness*. Because you've already connected everyone's purpose to this difficult project, they will be able to visualize the accomplishment and celebrate together—shared fate.

Healthy tension leads to a sense of shared fate. Stress leads to isolation and anxiety.

There will be tension, but tension is a good thing. It provides the adrenaline, excitement, and eagerness to accomplish and achieve. A healthy tension allows people to produce at a high level.

Tension can create a healthy sense of urgency, and with controls, that urgency propels people forward without the stress. Without controls—comprehension and commitment of the alignment between time, tasks, and purpose— urgency *can* be stressful. As the leader, you can manage the urgency so that it's created in a way that drives productivity without stress.

Meet as a Group

When you talk to your people about how their work aligns to purpose, do it with a group. Don't single people out. It's unlikely that just one person is struggling to connect their time and tasks to purpose, so it's better to explain it to the group as a whole. They'll be more open to asking questions and speaking with you and one another about how aligning time and tasks with purpose affects their jobs, so you can speak with them about that as a team. Use the creative energy of your team. They will feel more like they're taking this journey together instead of being left to figure it out on their own.

When you commit to having these conversations, you'll see firsthand what happens when you make purpose the boss and then let it do its job. Put purpose to work. Let it make the decisions. Listen to purpose and let it tell you what needs to be done next.

If anyone on your team does not understand how to align, or if alignment is even necessary, you'll need to have a one-on-one. Don't ignore it and think it will just work itself out. People who don't understand why they are doing what they are doing and when become disgruntled. Disgruntled employees are always unfulfilled. Take them back to step one so they understand the need to comprehend and commit to the changes and benefits aligning brings to the company and their personal and professional fulfillment.

Chapter 6 Summary and Application

Priority needs to be driven by purpose, *not* chaos. Shifting this mindset away from traditional management takes careful planning, time, and effort. You need to serve your people well through mindful preparation before you even start the process of prioritization.

Before you launch into prioritizing time and tasks, make it a point to first connect these tasks with the department and company purpose. Initially, this might seem overwhelming, but stay focused. Keep in mind that the hard work of aligning will ultimately lead to your people experiencing a sense of fulfillment rooted in purpose as they leave the office every day feeling like they won. When you get frustrated, motivate yourself by thinking about that fulfillment—it's happening slowly, but surely. Don't lose sight of the forest in the trees. Keep going.

When you make culture (purpose and principles) the boss, healthy tension takes the place of stress. Urgency doesn't ever go away, but these moments will be embraced rather than feared because your people will be motivated by something more. Instead of seeing a project as disconnected and then feeling stressed, they'll begin to see themselves as a valuable cog in a much larger gear. Through the lens of shared fate, they will start to understand what they are capable of.

Remember, this is *simple, not easy*. You must walk through the alignment process expecting it to test you. Don't assume that all of your employees will be able to immediately connect time and tasks to purpose. Be prepared to hold the banner of culture with confidence, making it the boss rather than you.

1. What does each marble in your jar represent?
2. What changes would have to take place to make those a priority?

3. How does healthy tension lead to a shared fate? Can you see how this would create worthwhile work?

4. List some ways you could use those priorities to manage the urgency and not give in to stress. Choose one of them to take action on this week.

Chapter 7

YOUR PRIORITIES

*People want to win at work. They crave
accomplishment and purpose. Prioritization
helps give that sense of achievement and,
ultimately, fulfillment to your people.*

B y this time, you've made culture (purpose and principles) the boss. As the leader, you have gotten
clarification between purpose and tasks so you can
explain it to your people. You've done that work because you
know it's worth doing. You want happy, fulfilled, productive
people—not stressed-out employees.

Your employees now have full clarity on who's in charge
and they're totally onboard. You've done all that work, and,

as a result, you've removed uncertainty and ambiguity from the workplace *and* removed the stress.

While the stress is gone, tension remains, but it's a *healthy* tension that provides the drive your people need to step into their work ethic and accomplish whatever needs to be done.

Get in Front of Your People

People need to understand what's going on and why it's happening. The way I typically begin this process is by going into a room with a team and having them identify every task they do every day. I start the conversation by stating the purpose. I remind them of the company's purpose and how the purpose of their role aligns. Then I write their tasks on a white board or put them up on a screen so everyone can see exactly what gets done every day by every member of that team.

This in and of itself is a powerful exercise. Your people will recognize how much work is being done by their team. You need to recognize this too. Tell them: *Look at what you guys do. That's amazing!*

We typically go through several iterations of identifying different tasks and sometimes we sort them by type of task, but we make sure every single task is included. We try to get it down to a very granular list—a very large, very detailed list of exactly what that team does.

I explain to my people that the job they have in this meeting is to begin identifying which tasks support the purpose and which ones do not. They also need to help me identify the priority of each task: which one needs to get done first, second, third, and so on.

Requirements, Needs, and Wants

As you work through this process with your team and you're identifying all the tasks, you are going to discover tasks that don't fit the purpose and need to be eliminated. Classify the rest into three categories: requirements, needs, and wants.

Requirement tasks include anything that has a hard deadline that's been set from outside the organization. An external audit, for example, would fit the requirement category, so any task that needs to be done to prepare for that audit would go into the requirement category. A project that's due to a client by a certain deadline would also be a requirement.

A *need* task addresses something that, if left undone, could introduce a threat to your company, such as loss of business or revenue. You need to make sure these tasks are completed, but if they're not, the business won't necessarily be shut down.

The *want* tasks are tasks that remain, and these are tasks that align with the purpose but aren't necessary—the "nice to haves." It would be nice to accomplish them, if and when someone has time to do them.

After you've decided whether each task is a requirement, a need, or a want, you can start prioritizing them, beginning with those in the requirement category. If there are thirty requirement tasks, you will work through them, numbering each one from one to thirty.

As you walk through this process, elicit your team's thoughts on how they believe each task should be prioritized. As the leader, you're there to ask a lot of *why* questions, understanding how the task and its priority relates back to the purpose. Continue this process through the needs and wants tasks.

This exercise will provide you with a lot of insight into what happens in your company. It will show you who does what—and who's excited to do more. People who clearly see the connection between tasks and purpose will be energized, and you'll feel that healthy tension in the room. They will want to do the work they see as being most impactful for the purpose.

To optimize this process, do it more than once. Revisit it whenever something changes, such as a new requirement coming up or a shift in purpose. Once your people understand it, let them lead these meetings while you stand aside to ask questions and make sure they're basing their decisions on the purpose. Review these tasks, at minimum, weekly to remind people *what* they need to be doing (task), *when* they need to be doing it (prioritizing), and *why* (purpose).

The added benefit to working through tasks this way is that you can now talk about them openly with your people without them feeling like you're checking up on them. The tasks are clear, and everyone understands their connection to the purpose. Make sure they are visible to everyone and update them every time they change. When you stop by someone's desk and ask, "What are you working on today?" they won't feel micromanaged. They'll be happy to tell you exactly what they're doing because they know that what they do serves the purpose, not you. You're not asking for selfish reasons or even as a boss. You're asking because you're all in this together and you, like them, are committed to your company's purpose.

Everything Gets a Priority

You'll discover that while you do this, there will be tasks that some people do and tasks those same people will never do. However, you still need to identify the priority of these tasks in relation to one another. Everybody needs to understand the overall priority so that as you come together as a team under the banner of your purpose, you can rally each other. If every task has the same priority, you create a polarizing situation. If a task has the same priority as another, people will feel like that other task is in competition with theirs and they will not rally around seeing it get done. Prioritizing all your time and tasks gives people a banner to flock to.

This prioritization is especially critical in times of crisis, such as when you're nearing an important deadline. If someone has fallen behind on a task that's high in priority, other people on the team can put their tasks aside to help that person complete their task. This is how people display that they understand how to prioritize tasks to the purpose—which is exactly what you want them to do. They will then begin to work as a team instead of as individuals who just happen to be working on the same project.

Don't be surprised if tasks appear that no one is currently doing yet still need to be done. In the process of prioritizing time and tasks, your people might bring an issue or an opportunity for improvement to your attention that you didn't know existed. You might have people in your company who have more client contact than you do or who are closer to product development than you are. No one has ever asked them to prioritize time and tasks in this manner before, so now that they have the chance and they're looking at the tasks that need to be done, they may be inspired to let you know about a task that no one does yet but should probably be added. It may require a higher priority than many of the tasks people are already doing. You don't want to dismiss this information. Encourage it and ask the person to help you connect it to the purpose.

As the leader, you will transition much of the prioritization process to your people, but you still need to be aware of everything that happens within your company that might cause you to revisit and revise the culture (purpose and principles) and the tasks that align with all of this. You need to discuss these things with other leaders in your company and bring them to your team so they can act on them appropriately.

Prioritizing time and tasks, just like creating and cultivating culture, is an ongoing process that never ends. Your company is always evolving, and your people—as they begin to reap the benefits of alignment—will want to evolve with it, so they can keep enjoying the sense of fulfillment and winning.

Bring Your People Along

People can become apathetic toward their tasks when they don't feel the connection between *what* they're doing and *why* they're doing it. Likewise, they can become emotionally attached to tasks they've been doing for a long time, even though a task may not be tied to their purpose.

As outlined in the previous chapter, you've talked to your people about purpose. Now, to cultivate culture, you have to talk to your people about how their tasks support that purpose—even the dull or difficult tasks they don't enjoy. *Especially* those tasks. You also have to talk to them about the tasks they've been doing for a long time that don't serve the company's purpose. You have to explain to people why they're not going to be doing those tasks anymore.

You can imagine how that's going to go and how those employees are going to feel. Hearing that these tasks they do, and probably do *well*, are no longer part of their job will, at first, cause some fear in your people. It will make them question their value to the company. As you're walking into this process of prioritizing time and tasks, you have to adopt a mentality that while you are the leader, *the culture is the boss*, and what you are doing is an act of service to your shared purpose. Having this conversation as an *act of service* positions you to walk your people through the whys behind what they are doing.

Chapter 7 Summary and Application

People *want* to win at work. They crave accomplishment and purpose. Prioritization helps give that sense of achievement and, ultimately, fulfillment to your people. By leading your people through prioritization in this way, you really are performing an act of love and service. If you only see it as a means to get things done, then you'll be shifting your people away from culture and away from fulfillment.

Prioritization begins by connecting your team to purpose and reminding them why their specific work and tasks matter. This is your chance to speak life and significance into each individual. Be present and don't miss this opportunity. You could change a tedious task into something that sparks true passion. Or, this process could lead you to realize that an employee sees a task as tedious because it doesn't align to their purpose. You then get to take that task off their plate and that weight off their shoulders so they can really focus on their purpose. This is the kind of employee fulfillment I keep talking about. This is why you need to strive for consistent commitment to each part of this process. Continue to prioritize time and tasks through the lens of aligning so that your employees feel known, heard, and valued.

You will be tempted to make shortcuts here and simply prioritize *for* your team, rather than *with* them. Remember, you cannot do this on your own. If your people aren't actively involved in the process, then you're not serving them through this—you're micromanaging. Give your employees a voice. Lead them to start connecting tasks to purpose on their own. You'll begin to see a transformation in your team as they go home each day feeling like they've accomplished something worthwhile.

1. Are you currently doing tasks that do *not* fit within your purpose?

2. Now that you understand the purpose and importance of prioritization, spend some time applying the prioritization process to your own tasks and responsibilities. First, write out every task. Second, group the tasks into requirements, needs, and wants. Third, assign tasks a numerical priority (first, second, third, etc.).

3. How did it go? Was it painful? Choose someone to share the results with this week.

Chapter 8

REMAIN STEADFAST

*If you have a love for people, you will push
for their fulfillment through transformation,
innovation, and achievement.*

A s you walk into this process of prioritizing, remember, as an act of service, the goal of identifying and prioritizing time and tasks is not to make people's lives easier, but to allow them to live out a part of their character that feels really good about their accomplishments. When you do this with alignment, you remove the distraction of the fear of the unknown. People know exactly what they're doing, when, and why, and they can move forward toward fulfillment.

Don't expect these conversations to go smoothly, especially at first. No doubt, you will have at least one employee who's been doing the same tasks for ten years. Now you're going to tell them why certain tasks don't need to be done, and they're going to feel threatened and afraid. They will question their value to the business. They'll think about all the time they've put into accomplishing these tasks that are suddenly worthless.

People will react, and not always favorably, but taking this approach of service positions you to discuss their responsibilities in a more proactive and positive way. You're not taking something away from them, but instead directing them toward something that increases their value. Going forward, everything they do will align with the purpose; they'll know why they're doing what they do, and they'll understand the value they bring to the company. In fact, this may be the first time they'll see their unique value add to the company because if their work hasn't been tied to the purpose, they haven't yet experienced true fulfillment in the workplace.

This is a conversation, not a speech. If you are doing this right, there will be a dialogue (not a monologue) with lots of questions. Confirm that people are following along. Ask them, *"Does this make sense to you guys? Do you see how this works? What questions do you have?"*

Involve them in the decisions too. Giving them ownership will go a long way toward alleviating their fears because you immediately show them that you value their input. Again, you're not there to tell them what to do—that's not your job. Your job in aligning is to connect the dots for them between what they do and when and why they are doing it.

This is the *work* part—the consistency you need to apply in cultivating culture. Sure, it would be so much easier to lock yourself in your office and just start putting numbers—and even names—on tasks. If you do that, you've completely defeated the purpose of step one. You did all that work to create culture and cultivate it, and now you're turning your back on it. For what? To save time? To be the hero? Trust me, locking yourself in your office does not save time, nor does it make you a hero. Your people will think they went through all that work of cultivating culture (purpose and principles) for nothing because their leader is back to being no more than a typical boss.

Instead, prepare to spend some serious time getting this worked out. Ask a lot of questions to bring everyone into the conversation and process. Every time you work through tasks, continue to ask, "*Does this task align with our purpose?*" People may not agree on the answer, so you will have to talk through it. Get to the truth and remove any questions or ambiguity around the answer. Unless a task truly aligns with the purpose, you cannot leave it out there for someone to do. As you come to tasks that don't align, but people don't want to give them up, don't resort to a position of authority. Remember, you are a servant leader and it's your job as the leader to connect their role to purpose. Restate the purpose and revisit the tasks they're currently doing and those they will be doing.

As you begin to identify tasks that people have emotional ties to, you're likely to get some negative reactions. People may respond with fear, frustration, and even outright anger. Accept their reactions. These are normal human reactions and you should not dismiss them. Accept them and address them. This is your chance with an act of service to help your people understand how these *new* tasks are tied to the purpose and why doing them will increase the employee's, the team's, and the department's value to the company. Aligning with that purpose not only makes them even more valuable, it will also help them achieve *fulfillment* in their work.

In these conversations, be on the lookout for compliance. Some people would rather go along to get along than have all their questions answered. These are the people who nod in agreement to everything you say. If they're staring blankly, they probably aren't even following along. If they appear to understand but aren't engaged, they're just agreeing. They're not committed. You really need them to *get* this—to fully comprehend and commit to making this work because you are rebuilding an organizational culture that will serve them better while serving the company.

What happens if you don't address these issues? If you let people leave the meeting compliant, they won't take the conversation seriously. They heard you talking about what they're supposed to be working on and they understand the priority, but the minute someone drops a new task on their desk, it will immediately rise to the top of their priority list.

For these reasons, your meeting to discuss tasks and prioritization could become two, three, or six meetings.

People are fulfilled when their work has purpose and they don't have to worry that their leader is going to come around the next day and tell them they've been working on the wrong task. That kills their enthusiasm and creates stress, cynicism, and a sense of futility. Futility can never lead to fulfillment. You will never engage someone's work ethic if they're stressed out or cynical toward their work. They need certainty to get there, to be able to dive in and fully produce without fear and to the best of their ability.

Passing the Torch

Eventually, your role as the leader will be to transition this process to your team. You do this not only for the growth and evolution of your people but to ensure that you multiply yourself to maintain and deepen the culture. Once they understand how their jobs align with the purpose, they should be able to make decisions based on purpose without you having to intervene or lead them in the process.

To get them there, practice the process with them. Choose a task and ask them to discuss it and how it aligns to the purpose. You need them to be able to show you how they walk the task back to purpose. If they can't do that, there's no deep-rooted belief in that purpose because deep-rooted belief in a purpose provides transformation, innovation, and achievement. If they can't get to those three things, then you have not yet instilled in them a belief in that purpose.

Those three things—transformation, innovation, and achievement—become the litmus test from here on out. If you've done well in step one, test yourself throughout steps two, three, and four by looking for those three traits. If they don't exist throughout the next three steps, you've got to circle back and continue to build out a deeper understanding of this culture—your purpose and your principles. That cycle needs to be continuous.

If they are able to first assign purpose to tasks, then ask your people to prioritize tasks through categorizing them into requirements, needs, and wants. Once they can verbalize both how purpose connects to tasks, as well as prioritization, consider the torch to be passed to that person.

Chapter 8 Summary and Application

Prioritizing our time requires us to prioritize our tasks. This models to your team how to value time. You owe it to yourself and your team to take control of your most precious commodity: time. Fulfillment depends on your ability to understand what to do next. Without prioritizing your time, you are doomed to live in regret.

By now, I hope you've realized why step one, **create culture**, is crucial to the process of aligning. You can't achieve employee fulfillment if your employees are not first connected with a culture built firmly on purpose and guiding principles. And if you as a leader are not consistently tying everything back to culture, then you aren't fostering commitment within your people. Instead, you're communicating that compliance is enough. Compliance will never move your people toward fulfillment. If you have a love for people, you will push for their fulfillment through transformation, innovation, and achievement.

This is where your grit and strength of will really kick in. You have to be tireless and unwavering in your dedication. When you feel resistance from your people, remember the fulfillment you want for them and fight for it by embracing these tough conversations. If someone is upset about losing a task, it's easy to let your emotions take control. You'll feel tempted to respond with irritation and authority or fear and submission. But when you take it personally and respond with emotion, you're making this about yourself, *not* your people's fulfillment. Remember, this isn't personal. Recognize where that pushback is coming from—a disconnection from their purpose. Take up the banner of culture and lead your team by connecting tasks to purpose. *Simple, not easy.*

The hard work of prioritization lies in your ability as a leader to give your employees the permission and inspiration to prioritize for themselves. This is the difference between labor and leadership. If you still think your job is to tell people what to do, then you haven't been paying attention. Lead your people through prioritization until they can consistently tie tasks back to purpose by themselves and then *let them own it*. This is a step on the path to fulfillment for your people. This is what makes prioritization on the path to alignment so different from traditional management. When you practice this to its fullest, you're passing the torch of purpose to your employees and handing them the key to their fulfillment.

1. What do you think you could do better to ensure your people understand how to identify which tasks are priority?

2. In prioritization, the conversation is key. How do you recognize whether your team members are compliant, emotionally attached, or apathetic toward a task?

3. When prioritizing tasks with your team, how can you gauge transformation, innovation, and achievement? How does this look different for each of your team members?

4. Choose a person in your sphere of influence this week. Ask them questions to discover their priorities. How did this help you better understand their worldview?

KYLE'S STORY: PART TWO

Although Kyle was starting to understand that fulfillment was possible, he was not yet done overcoming obstacles and insecurities he carried from his previous work experiences. These obstacles and insecurities exist for most employees. The reality is that everyone wants to work hard and feel like that hard work matters. They don't want to waste time. Kyle was a remote employee who had to manage his own time and would be tempted to live in constant anxiety if he wasn't managing his time well. The work that was put in with Kyle to establish the purpose of his role allowed him to confidently move through each day. This doesn't mean that he didn't have questions, but because he believed so deeply in the purpose, he would get the clarity he needed.

Kyle knew firsthand from his past job what it feels like to waste your time. He worked on what he thought was the right task at the right time. Unfortunately, the previous organization did not have a clear, singular purpose to help guide him.

I quickly noticed Kyle prioritizing his time regularly and knew that despite being new to the organization, he was determined to leverage his time for our purpose. Six weeks later, I asked him to join me in leadership, and for the first time, the idea of leadership didn't spark fear and anxiety in Kyle. He was motivated and excited to be part of something greater than himself— to love and serve others toward their fulfillment. It pushed him to transcend the boundaries of what he thought was possible for himself as a leader.

Step Three

CREATE VALUE

Create value based on using an employee's soft skills over hard skills when assigning tasks. When employees take on tasks that they want to do instead of tasks they're willing to do, it will lead to fulfillment.

Chapter 9

VALUE SOFT SKILLS OVER HARD SKILLS

In the process of aligning, the only valuable hard skills are those born of a person's soft skills.

In traditional management, the boss spends a lot of time creating value in the eyes of their boss or in the eyes of their employees by celebrating their knowledge, achievement, and experience—this is not the value I am talking about. Our value as leaders comes from our ability to love and serve our people toward fulfillment. So, what do I mean by "create value?" I mean that we have to create value in our people through *our* eyes.

When I talk about creating value, I am not saying that we have to instill value in our people; instead, we need to recognize it, celebrate it, and leverage it. Leveraging their value is not self-serving when we leverage it for the purpose we all believe in. So then, what is this value I am talking about? I am talking about a human being's intrinsic value. That's right; it's already there. You just need to look for it.

Specifically, one of the ways this value shows up is in the form of soft skills. The way I define a soft skill is an inherent part of who you are that enables you to interact effectively and harmoniously with other people. If you have taken the time to create guiding principles (or core values), then you should already be able to recognize some of these soft skills.

Another way this value manifests is through your people's interests and passions. I use both of those words because depending on the level of trust you have with your people, they may shy away from talking about their passions but will feel free to talk about the things that interest them. The ultimate goal is to build that trust in a way that will compel them to share the things they are truly passionate about. When you take the time to recognize, celebrate, and leverage their value (soft skills, interests/passions), you are truly creating value not only in your eyes but also in the eyes of your clients and the entire organization.

The Trap

Your next job in aligning is to evaluate your human resources to ensure you have the right people working on the prioritized tasks. You do this by first looking at soft skills. As a leader, it's easy to assume that the team you inherited or the team you built prior to going through the alignment process is the right team for all those tasks you identified and prioritized. Evaluating your people is a continuous process so you can execute those tasks and live out your purpose.

In my career, there was a point where my business grew by 25 percent in just three months. Immediately, I felt gripped by fear, anxiety, and pressure—fear of failing to meet our new client's demands, anxiety about where to start, and pressure to quickly solve our lack of resources. Like many other leaders, I thought that the only solution to this burst in growth was to simply add more people, so I jumped to hire five more employees as soon as I could.

Throughout the hiring process, I was focused solely on hard skills. I brought people onboard who were very experienced account representatives and could technically do the tasks well, but I didn't spend any time considering or evaluating their soft skills. Because I put hard skills first, I wasn't upholding our culture above everything else. As a result, all five of those employees resigned in less than two years, which in turn sparked and spread fear in my people and my clients. This seemingly minor decision to value hard skills set off a ripple effect that first fractured and then shattered our culture.

That ripple caused me and my people to lose all we had worked to build in our culture and its recovery and restoration set us back an entire year. I realized that we lost that time specifically because of the neglect of soft skills in hiring. We needed a shift in our approach. We needed to go back to the drawing board and start assessing and emphasizing soft skills.

Focus on Soft Skills

The conventional way to look at human resources—your people—is by focusing on their hard skills. This is what most leaders and recruiters do. When we do this, we miss out on a major component of who people are. An individual's soft skills can have much greater value, yet they are so often overlooked. The only valuable hard skills are those born of a person's soft skills.

Let me explain. We define a hard skill as something that can be taught and is measurable. Soft skills, on the other hand, are those intangible components of a person's character. Soft skills identify who a person *is* or who they *choose to be* as opposed to the information they choose to learn. **A person's soft skills will enhance their hard skills.**

Let's say one of your people is really good at spreadsheets. This person puts together payroll reports and they are very good at creating formulas in Excel to help you make decisions around payroll. That's an example of a hard skill. It's one that might be replaced by software. This is not to diminish the value of hard skills. They're very important, but a hard skill on its own is far less valuable than when it comes out of a person's soft skill.

This same person has the soft skill of wanting to ensure data integrity in all their work. You probably know someone like that. Data integrity matters to this person so much that they're going to take special care to make sure all their Excel formulas are right and useful to your decision-making. This individual is the exact person you want managing the spreadsheets, not only because they excel at Excel, but because the accuracy of the data *matters* to them. The data integrity of those spreadsheets is perhaps even more important to them than finishing the task. Therefore, what you get out of that report will be far more valuable because it came out of someone's soft skill—that desire for integrity and accuracy—than if it were just a task they had learned. Who would you rather have doing your payroll spreadsheets—the person with good Excel skills or the person with good Excel skills *and* a passion for integrity?

The individual with the hard skill that is not born out of a soft skill will do the task, but their motivation is different. They're trying to complete a task. The other person is trying to do the task to the best of their ability to *satisfy something within themselves.*

This idea of hard skill versus soft skill is a concept that you, the leader, need to understand. Remember how we talked about the idea that the motivation you need to do the hard work of aligning must come from a love for people? This is where that belief really manifests itself. If you truly care about your people, you will seek to assign them work they care about. This shows your people that you value them for who they are and want to become, instead of looking at them only for what they can do for you.

Soft Skills to Guiding Principles

When you begin evaluating people for soft skills to match them with tasks they care about, you'll probably discover some skills that are so attractive—and would be a valued skill in any employee—that you decide to adopt them as a guiding principle.

For example, a woman who really loves to learn new things joined our team. She came in not knowing all the skills to fully function in her role, but she was open and honest about what she did and did not know and she was eager to learn. She wanted to *learn with humility*. This wasn't a skill that she learned in a classroom. She perhaps developed the skill through personal experiences. Those experiences had instilled in her this unique skill that benefited her in any role she took on.

Not everyone can start a new job or take on a new role and hit the ground running on their first day. But ask yourself this: Would you rather hire a person who believes they know everything about a task and does not want to learn anything new or a person who is honest about their knowledge and can't wait to learn all that you will teach them?

We've all been on a team with somebody new who just wants to start applying their hard skills before they are a learner. They don't really want to learn about the team, the purpose, what we're trying to accomplish, or what people have done in the past. They only want to prove their value by applying their hard skill on day one.

We recognized the soft skill of learning with humility was so valuable that we made it one of our guiding principles. Not all soft skills will become guiding principles, but all your guiding principles should be soft skills by which you evaluate new hires.

Recruit So You Can Avoid Hiring

Don't wait for the need to recruit to force you to hire. You "hire" hard skills but "recruit" soft skills. That means that the process of adding people to your team or organization is best served through a recruitment mindset. The most effective way to recruit is to build a large referral network. To build this network, multiply yourself by leveraging anyone in your sphere of influence, personal or professional, who understands the culture you're trying to cultivate. When you've adopted that mindset, you engage your army of recruiters to identify people they know will add value to you, not just your organization.

Look for people who align with your guiding principles. This alignment comes through examining both written and verbal communication to identify whether their focus is primarily on hard skills or soft skills. If the vast majority of communication revolves around hard skills, then they probably believe that the majority of their value comes from what they do and not who they are.

Find people with interests/passions that can align to your company's purpose. It's not that you would disqualify someone because, on the surface, you don't see how their interests/passions connect with your purpose, but you definitely want to make it a priority to vet that out. Due diligence will help you determine if they are interested in the job or in the company's purpose.

Referrals need to be procured over time. In other words, this must be an ongoing focus—a new mindset. If you're not being proactive with recruiting by building a referral network, then you are not preparing for inevitable turnover and/or growth. Create a game plan to identify people who will be a value add to your company. Don't wait for the need to recruit to force you to hire.

Hard Choices Around Hard Skills

As I mentioned earlier, after that season of rapid growth, I made decisions that affected the culture. I brought new people in and didn't worry about whether their beliefs aligned with our guiding principles. I put their soft skills aside and just hired them quickly to do the work—and didn't worry about how they fit, how much they cared about the work, and how fulfilled they would be.

If you have been or are currently in this position, I get it. I've been there before. I can tell you that making that desperate decision simply to take the pressure off was the wrong decision. If you go that route, you'll be dealing with the fallout later.

First off, the quality of the work will not be as good if you have not connected their value to that task. You should have already established that the task is important by connecting it to purpose, so now it is time to unleash your people. If their beliefs don't align with your culture, that will cause even bigger issues. Finally, think about how your decision affects everyone else.

The irony of hiring simply for hard skills is that leaders often think this is the most efficient and effective way to go. They expect high value and productivity to be the outcome of their decision. The truth is, they end up sacrificing product and service quality. They also show everyone else on their team that they're not serious about the culture or about employee fulfillment. This will have an adverse effect on the productivity and morale of the team and possibly other teams that interact with that team. People will see that purpose and principles don't really matter as much as they were led to believe, or as much as they once did, and they'll begin to check out. That enthusiasm you all worked so hard to develop will wither away.

The same is true if you allow people to remain on your team based solely on their mastery of a hard skill. For example, you might have somebody on your team who can do a particular hard skill in their sleep. However, they will only do it alone, and they have no interest in sharing the task with another person, even though one of your guiding principles is *teamwork*. They believe that their mastery of a particular hard skill makes them so valuable to the company that the teamwork value doesn't apply to them. This won't work. They'll get the job done, but they will be misaligned with their team and it will affect everyone around them. You will not be able to sustain alignment if you send the message that individuals with the right hard skills don't have to share the culture (purpose and principles) that everyone else lives by.

Another issue this creates is that this person will never find fulfillment in their work. If they are gauging their value simply by their ability to do a task, they'll be fearful that eventually another team member or a software application will come in and do a job better than they can.

In contrast, the application of a soft skill that reflects each person's uniqueness cannot be replicated by anyone else.

Chapter 9 Summary and Application

This step of creating value pushes you to ensure that not only do you have *enough* resources, but you also have the *right* resources to accomplish your purpose. Notice I said accomplish your *purpose*, not your tasks. Being rooted in purpose is what makes the process of aligning so different and so much more than traditional management. Purpose is what leads to your people's fulfillment, and that fulfillment stems out of their soft skills. If you continue to focus on achievement through hard skills instead of fulfillment through soft skills, all of your efforts will be for nothing.

Hard skills require information; soft skills require transformation.

A hard skill is something that's measurable and can be taught. That's not to say hard skills aren't valuable—they are—but they definitely aren't *more* valuable than soft skills. Building a team that's committed to cultivating the culture through the pursuit of purpose starts with understanding your people's soft skills. They're part of what drives your team to accomplish purpose in the first place. They're also much more difficult to learn or teach because they're an integral part of *who somebody is.*

Imagine your team's purpose is to serve people and you want to hire someone who knows how to use Excel. You could easily train this person to use Excel, but how can you measure the amount of time it would take to instill in them the importance of serving people? Would it even be possible? If you choose to hire someone based solely on their hard skills in Excel, then they would eventually be unfulfilled in their work and your team would never achieve its purpose.

Now imagine someone currently on your team whose soft skills are being leveraged for their tasks. They come into work energized and inspired because they believe that the work they do matters. Because they're so deeply invested in their work, the quality of what they do improves. They truly thrive because they get to live out their passion every single day.

This is why it's critical to make sure your people are personally connected to the work they do. Don't make the same mistake I did in hiring people for what they can do rather than who they are. You'll lose all you've worked for if you choose to abandon culture in favor of bringing someone in quickly just to get the job done. People deserve to be passionately connected to their work. Your "no" to a hard skills hire is a "yes" to protecting your company's culture.

1. What is your value? Without using hard skills, describe what makes you valuable to your team.

2. Historically, how much emphasis have you placed on soft skills?

3. What soft skills are you looking for?

4. Pick someone on your team this week. Communicate their value to you, both personally and professionally.

Chapter 10

DISCOVER YOUR PEOPLE

*A person's life experiences often dictate
their personal passions—what they
want to be doing to feel fulfilled.*

Y
ou need to align your people with the right tasks.
You need to go a little bit deeper with your people
to discover what interests them. What are their
interests or passions? What are the tasks that have been
prioritized, that people look at thinking, *I would really love
to do that*?

Leverage your people's interests to do a task in order to
take that task to the next level. This is something you can
begin in a group setting, but you'll also need to go through

the process with your people one-on-one. Even though one of your team members has an interest in the task, they might not volunteer because they don't feel like they have the appropriate hard skill. Let's say you have a project to update a website. They might feel too self-conscious to say out loud, "I would really love to work on the website" when there are two web designers sitting in the room. As a leader, don't assume that just because the web designers have the hard skill to design a website, they are required to own all related tasks.

Every hard skill on the planet can be taught. No one is born a brain surgeon or a rocket scientist. No one is born a web designer either. These roles require a lot of information and training. It sure helps if the person who trains to be a brain surgeon is passionate about biology, physiology, and people and that the rocket scientist has a passion for science, math, and astronomy. More than likely, their life experiences created an interest that eventually evolved into a passion. A person's life experiences often dictate their personal passions—what they want to be doing to feel fulfilled.

Figure Out What People *Want* to Do, Not What They're *Willing* to Do

Figuring out what people want to do can be difficult. In the workplace, employees are not likely to let you know what they want to do. They are much more likely to let you know what they're *willing* to do. That may be a good job security strategy, but they will never be fulfilled at work with that mentality.

When I first began this task at my company, I had a meeting with the marketing team to do an initial discovery around which tasks interested people. As I pointed to a task, people were giving me the same responses: *Yeah, I can do that. I'm willing to do that. I'll take that on. That's something that I can do.*

I had to stop and explain, "Okay, I get that. I know you guys are all good people who are willing to take on whatever needs to be done because you believe in the purpose, but that doesn't help me here. What do you *want* to do? Also, what do you *not* want to do?"

Once they understood what I was asking from them, people began speaking up. "Well, you know, actually I don't like to work on video editing."

"Perfect," I said, "This is a start."

Now I had a decision to make. I could continue making this person do a task I knew wasn't their favorite. This could mean the employee would always be wanting to do something else, maybe *somewhere else*. Instead, I could discover what they *wanted* to do. Each individual needs to serve something within themselves as well.

Again, people typically won't express interest in a task that someone else is already doing, especially if they're doing it really well. They'll be afraid people might be dismissive, or they might be afraid that the person who's already doing it will feel threatened, like they're trying to take their job away from them.

But guess what? The person doing that task might actually welcome the opportunity to have that person learn it. Maybe this person has always wanted to mentor someone and has never had the chance because no one else wanted to learn the job. Or maybe this person is tired of doing this particular task and would really like a shot at something else. People are typically not going to volunteer this kind of information, which is why you will have to make your expectations clear: You *really* want to know what they want to do!

Empowering your people to express which tasks they want to do is helpful because there are people who would love to do something but are afraid to speak up. Someone might say, "I've always wanted to learn video editing. Do you think this is a task I could have if someone would teach it to me?"

This is an exciting moment, so pay attention. One of your people has just expressed interest in a new task. This is your cue.

This is Personal

You're learning about everyone's interests and passions and the tasks they would like to take on. You're stepping them through the connection between each task and purpose and ensuring they fully understand how what they want to do aligns with your company's purpose. The next task for you is to decide—together—who does what.

This won't happen in a day, and it may not happen in a month. It's a discovery process that will take many conversations to understand your people's interests and, eventually, passions. You might need to speak with one individual several times to get them to open up about what they want to do and why.

Put yourself in their place for a moment to understand why they may not want to tell you about their interests. Right now, they have a job. They fill a role and have tasks they have proven they can do. Talking to you about other tasks they might have interest in seems risky. What if you don't want them to do that task? What if you misunderstand them and think they're just unhappy working on their current tasks or even on the company purpose? Anything they tell you beyond "I love what I do and here is what else I'm willing to do" could be seen as a huge risk in their eyes.

You must continuously develop a trusting relationship with your people and help them understand your intentions—to lead them toward fulfillment. As you establish trust with your people, not only will they be willing to share their interests, but they will also start to share their passions. Make these conversations a safe place for your people to open up and they will talk.

You're figuring out which of the tasks that you've identified and prioritized together is a good fit for what excites them. You're letting them know you want them to have the chance to learn the task *and* contribute to the purpose in the process.

Chapter 10 Summary and Application

In chapter one, I shared that two-thirds of people feel unfulfilled by their work. But you *can* make an impact and change this by getting to know your people and finding out what tasks and interests drive them.

The good news is that if you as the leader have done the hard work of cultivating your company's culture, then you *already* have people who are deeply connected to the purpose and committed to the guiding principles. This commitment, paired with the right tasks, leads to an employee who is driven, passionate, and alive in the workplace and beyond. Don't pass up the chance to be a part of it.

People are naturally hardwired for growth. This means that, eventually, *everyone* in your company will be looking for more—more challenges, more opportunities, more innovation. Your people *will* outgrow their tasks and strive for more. Anticipate this and be ready for it. Discovering your people is one way to protect your purpose and ensure it's achieved, but it's also a way to create value and worth in your employees. Honor your people by expecting them to not only grow more but also to *ask* for more. Empower them to voice which tasks energize them and which ones drain them.

This requires a massive shift from the typical thought process of traditional management. How often do people get to talk so openly about their interests with their leader? Discovering your people in this way *will* be hard. They'll likely be scared or resistant to share openly and honestly about tasks they don't like or the new ones they want to learn. Putting themselves out there is a huge risk for them personally *and* professionally. But if your motivation is rooted in loving and serving people, you'll alleviate that anxiety and encourage authenticity instead. If you're only motivated by your own achievement, title, salary, or success, then you'll never truly live out this process of alignment. You have to be committed to cultivating an environment built on trust. If your people trust you and feel safe with you, then sharing their thoughts and ideas about their tasks will happen instinctively.

1. Think of a time you shared your ambitions and dreams with someone in authority. Can you recall how that felt?

2. Think about a time when someone went from "having to do" to "wanting to do" something. What did you observe about that experience?

3. How are you engaging with your people to identify their interests?

4. What are some ways you can create or cultivate a work environment safe enough for your people to share their dreams and express their discontent?

5. Test your theories. Choose a person in your sphere of influence this week to listen to and understand their level of trust in the relationship.

Chapter 11

TASK ALIGNMENT AND ASSIGNMENT

*You'll always feel the pressure of looming
deadlines to skip necessary conversations,
but it's crucial to your people's fulfillment
to take the time.*

At this point, you've identified all the tasks that need
to be done. You've eliminated unnecessary ones,
added new ones, and categorized them all into
requirements, needs, and wants. You have tied them all back
to the purpose of the company, the department, and the
team. You've had conversations with your team and with

individuals to discover their soft skills and also to find out what they want to do and don't want to do. You've also identified some mentoring opportunities among your people and realized there may be some gaps.

Now you need a practical way to make allocating your human resources a reality.

Engage Your Team

You must distribute tasks *with* your people. Doing it on your own from an authoritarian role will rob your people of feeling any ownership in the decision and the tasks they take on. They need to be involved, and it's up to you to invite them into that discussion.

You might think you're setting yourself up for a difficult conversation. You have all these tasks and all your people, and it seems unlikely that you'll be able to perfectly match them up—especially if you involve your people in the decision. The two biggest problems that could come up are that you might have a task *everyone* wants to do. At the other extreme, you might have a task *no one* wants to do.

In the early phases of these conversations, it may take longer to get your team to decide how to distribute their tasks. As the leader, you may also feel the weight of urgent deadlines, stress, or pressure to just keep doing business as usual. Remember: This is *simple, not easy,* and it *will* test your patience. Don't fall into the trap of going down the path of least resistance. Allow your team and yourself the time and space to get this right. You can't cut any corners, especially when it comes to the investment of time. If you don't put in the hours to work through it, the short-term success of quickly completing projects will cost you the growth of your people.

Remind yourself often of the leader you're trying to become. You have to choose if you want to just get things done or if you want true fulfillment for your people. Aligning is about fulfillment through transformation. Transformation requires change, and change is *hard*.

The Task Everyone Wants to Do

When working through task alignment and assignment, you'll be faced with tasks multiple people want to do. This is a situation I've dealt with many times before. In one instance, I had three people who wanted to do the same task. Of the three, one of them had been doing it for years, while the other two had never done it.

I started by asking each of them to talk about the purpose of their role—how they can best put their passions to work to support their team's and the company's purpose. I asked them to describe how the tasks they're *currently doing* fulfilled that purpose and how the task they *wanted to do* would fulfill it. This was a critical moment. I needed to make sure my people could walk each task back to purpose. Having practiced many times, my employees were well-versed in connecting their tasks to the purpose of their role. If they couldn't make the connection, then they shouldn't be taking on this task, and we could then decide who should be assigned to it based on their exploration of purpose.

After discussing each person's thoughts on the connection to purpose, I then encouraged them to talk about their *personal* attachment to that task. It's vital to encourage your people to examine this feeling. They need to tell their team why they want to do this. They need to discuss it openly and honestly and really own their decision to want the task.

As you're having these conversations, people may realize the task doesn't suit their soft skills, or they may discover they really don't have the passion to do it after all. If doing the task requires them to give up a task they love (passion) or is natural to them (soft skills), they may change their mind about it.

If after this discussion you still have three people wanting the same task, it's up to you as the leader to come up with a solution that works for everyone. In my case, we decided that the person who currently did the task would now do it every Monday, Wednesday, and Friday. On Tuesdays and Thursdays, that person would mentor the other two on how to do it. Eventually, this opened up time for the person who had been doing the task to take on *new* tasks—tasks that suited their soft skills, supported the purpose of their role, and that they really *wanted to do* but never had time for.

Be sure to keep a keen eye on people's reactions to what others are saying. You may have team members who go along to get along, but they're really not pleased with the decision.

Don't ignore that—address it. If you gloss over it and think the person will somehow become happy with the decision, you're kidding yourself.

Let them know that it doesn't seem like they're in agreement and the only way for all of you to move forward as a team is if everyone is thrilled with the direction you're taking. If there are objections, get them out in the open and discuss them. This may entail a follow-up, one-on-one discussion with a team member.

It's so tempting to take the easy way out and ignore someone's displeasure with a decision in the workplace, but that displeasure won't go away. It will always be the elephant in the room. **When aligning, don't ignore the elephant— talk about it all the time.** We get all those things out in the open that might prevent people from being fulfilled.

If you've created a culture where people trust each other, anyone experiencing discomfort should be able to tell you why. The information they have could be very useful. For example, someone may not be excited about a task, but they also don't want to hand it to another person. When they speak to you privately, you might discover their apprehension isn't based on a resistance to teamwork or any other reason that doesn't align with the company's principles. They may be able to tell you why they are struggling. They understand the complexity of the task and how it connects to the purpose of their role. Because of this understanding, one of their soft skills shows up in the form of being very conscientious.

Their concern of re-assigning the task is only because it is a relatively new team member who may not have the experience to understand the complexity and importance of the task. This team member truly *believes* in what they are doing.

Let this person know that you understand their perspective and want to work toward a solution by discussing it with the person who may take the task on in the future. Again, work to find an outcome that will be a win-win for everyone. As long as both people are rallied behind the purpose, they'll be okay with this decision.

Traditional management teaches us that decisions usually result in team members either being compliant or rebellious. Don't let all the work you've put into aligning with your team go to waste by making assumptions about their reaction to a decision—believe the best about your people. Be humble enough to discuss the elephant in the room in a way that creates buy-in to the best idea; you may be right, but without buy-in, you will always be alone.

On the other hand, you may find out the reason someone's not happy with a decision is due to a personal agenda, such as a greater title or more compensation. In that case, you will need to address it. Alignment cannot coincide with personal agendas—it relies on purposed agendas to succeed.

The Task No One Wants to Do

There will inevitably be a task that *everyone* hates. This is an uncomfortable and difficult thing for a leader to navigate, even more so than when everyone enjoys a task. You can't go right back into traditional management of immediately assigning the task. You also can't just give your people what they want. Because you want fulfillment to be realized as quickly as possible, you'll yet again be tempted to take the path of least resistance. Resist that urge. You can't bypass your efforts to reach fulfillment for your people and yourself. This will take time and requires your strength of will.

Keep in mind that the focus of this conversation will always depend on your team's valuable input, so don't expect the same outcome every time. It will evolve as you and your people do.

To guide you and your team through assigning the task no one wants to do, first review the broader company purpose all the way down to each person's purpose. Remember, connect the task to the purpose. Remind them that everybody believes in accomplishing the purpose and this task is a necessary step.

Once everyone is on the same page, then figure out why no one likes to do it. Is it the way it's being done? Is it the technology (or lack thereof) being used to accomplish it? Find out what the struggle is and look for opportunities for innovation—remember, alignment always leads to transformation, innovation, and achievement. **This is a conversation, not a dictation.** Listen to what your people have to say. If they tell you the software that they're using is extremely slow, which causes a delay in getting a report done quickly, someone else in the room may have an idea for another way to get that report—innovation. Give them that platform to work through solutions instead of giving up.

If you still haven't found a way to assign the task, you now need to appeal to the value that you have created by highlighting your people's soft skills and passions. Leverage this value for what it is, the ability of human beings to accomplish even the least enjoyed task by applying their passion and soft skills to something greater than themselves—purpose. We are going to agree together that is not a task that is fun and exciting, but that is necessary, so you need someone to apply their dedication (soft skill) to this task.

Crisis State Versus Steady State

There may be times when you need to make decisions and your preferred method of task assignment just won't work. You'll have a task that needs to be done right away and a person with the hard skill to accomplish it.

Talk about the situation with your team. Let them know the circumstances and explain to them that you may have to override the way you typically operate. These are emergency-type situations where the business could be impacted (this is a required task) if you wait to get someone on a task whose soft skills and/or passions are a great match, but they don't have the hard skills yet.

Let your people know this is a temporary situation and, once that emergency passes, you will go back to getting a person on the task who really wants to do it.

Circumstances might require this action, and as long as you have the discussion with your people about what is going to happen and why, they will be onboard and won't feel like they've been tricked into believing you're committed to aligning only when it's convenient.

Traditionally, leaders know when to re-assign people in times of crisis, but they seldom take the time to let their people know *why*. They skip the conversation, which can literally take just five minutes of getting everyone in a room. Neglecting to bring your people along leaves the person who *was* doing the task feeling like they're failing. It can make the person you're putting back on the task feeling frustrated because you told them they were off that task and now you're pulling them back in.

This is simple, not easy. That extra few minutes to have the conversation will sustain everything you're trying to accomplish. You'll feel the pressure of looming deadlines to skip the conversation, but it's crucial to your people's fulfillment to take that time.

The conversation might go like this: "Hey, listen everyone. This client just called, and they need this report by the end of the day. It's a complex report that John has done in the past, and Sam hasn't been trained on it yet. Best case scenario is that John could train Sam on it today, but this is a rush job and we don't have the luxury of time. John's going to jump in and get it done, then they'll both go back to their new roles and tasks, the ones we all decided to take on."

If at all possible, Sam should shadow John as a quick training on the task. That way the report would get done on time and Sam would have some initial training on it. He and John might set up a second training for the following week when they could take their time and go through all the details. Maybe Sam will take on a task of documenting the process for creating the report during the training. But for today, due to the circumstances, the main priority is that John gets the report done right and on time.

The difference between these approaches is the communication between leader and team. Taking the time to communicate the decisions you make and why you're making them goes a long way toward ensuring the comprehension and commitment you need for alignment.

_____

Chapter 11 Summary and Application

Are you understanding why I keep saying this is *simple, not easy*? You'll constantly be faced with challenges that require you to make intense shifts in the fundamentals of how you work and think. Now you're immersed in the work of task alignment and assignment.

You'll be tempted to assign tasks *for* people, rather than letting your people do it as a team. You'll also be tempted to assign these tasks according to hard skills rather than softs skills just to get the job done. The way you've done it in the past won't work here. Alignment is about employee fulfillment, and a step on the path to that fulfillment is allowing your people to be involved in what they do every day.

You'll inevitably face changes in priorities along the way, and as priorities change, so will tasks. When your people are part of what they're doing and fully understand how it points back to cultivating culture, they'll feel less frustrated when those priorities shift because they can understand the reasons *why*. Don't ever skip the valuable and crucial opportunity to bring them along.

As a leader, be prepared for tough conversations and moments of tension with your people. These conversations usually arise from tasks everyone wants to do and tasks no one wants to do. Remember, the elephant in the room should never be ignored—you *always* talk about it. You can't view these conversations as negative. Look at them as opportunities for building trust, working together as a team, and engaging everyone in problem-solving their way back to purpose. The critical role you play as a leader is to ensure that everyone is connected to purpose through their belief. Leverage the value each team member brings (soft skills and passions) to take on every task. Throughout this, you also need to ask thoughtful questions to discover why your people are responding a certain way. Pay attention. What's their body language saying? Do they seem excited when they talk about a certain task? Be present so that you can gauge whether they're compliant or committed. Stick with it until you're confident everyone is aligned.

Urgency and deadlines don't ever go away. There will be times when you absolutely have to assign someone who has the hard skills to accomplish the task. But you can still practice alignment in these moments by communicating with your people. Let them in on the *why*, and you won't lose any momentum in maintaining culture and pushing for fulfillment for your people.

1. How would you navigate a conversation regarding a task no one wants to do? A task everyone wants to do?

2. Oftentimes, people bury their frustration with a decision made in the workplace. When this isn't discussed head-on, it becomes an elephant in the room. Going forward, how do you plan to address the elephant in the room?

3. What conversations have you been avoiding because of urgent deadlines, stress, or pressure to keep doing business as usual?

4. Identify a conversation that must happen this week.

KYLE'S STORY: PART THREE

Kyle had finally found that he wasn't afraid of leadership anymore. Every day, he was discovering and experiencing the benefits of alignment. Kyle's soft skills really began to shine, and he continually built on his confidence in exploring how his passions aligned to our purpose. This naturally led him to not only pursue his leaders for alignment and, ultimately, fulfillment, but it also led to him helping his peers do the same. He kept working on and improving the process of aligning tasks with his people. Kyle never stopped asking questions of his leaders and inviting them to challenge his thought process. He continued to do so because he wasn't just serving himself anymore; he was serving his team. He was living out his soft skills of kindness and learning with humility while also serving our purpose.

I saw Kyle prioritize his team's time, as well as assign tasks to his people based on their passions and soft skills. He knew how to connect tasks to purpose in a meaningful way for his team. I knew that I wanted that same experience for a greater number of my employees. At the time, I didn't even have a position that fit exactly what would suit his passion and soft skills. I sat down with my team and we decided to create a brand-new position just for him. Creating this position for Kyle was a win for everyone. Not only was this a huge opportunity for him to serve our purpose through his soft skills in a more influential way, but it was also an opportunity for my company to be better because Kyle was experiencing fulfillment. His pursuit of alignment and fulfillment had opened up a path to transformation for both of us.

EVERYONE HAS INTRINSIC VALUE

It is important to recognize and celebrate your value as well as everyone on your team. I define that value by your soft skills and your passions. Here are some tools that can help you recognize this value.

UNLOCK YOUR LEADERSHIP SUPERPOWER

Discover your leadership superpower by recognizing the soft skills you already live out on a daily basis. In order for this to be a true superpower, you have to believe that is holds value.

YOUR PASSION DISCOVERY PROCESS

Your passions combine your worldview and the strength of your will. Together, it creates an unstoppable force within every person to accomplish great things. Discover your passions, embrace them, and learn how to leverage them.

Visit alignleadthrive.com/align for resources to help you identify your leadership superpower and tools to dive deeper into your people!

Step Four

CREATE SUCCESS

As you start to create value in your eyes around your people, you won't be able to stop yourself from imagining how they can play a bigger role in accomplishing a purpose. Watching them apply their value as a human being to the purpose and guiding principles will lead you to see them for who they are—you will recognize their greatness.

Chapter 12

REIMAGINE THE FUTURE

Pursue your people and do it on purpose.

nvesting in your people through continual alignment will always yield a great ROI. That's right— a return on investment. In this chapter, I am going to define what this return will look like. By aligning your people to the culture that we have defined and are cultivating through our individual beliefs, we've identified the participants for this journey. We have established our destination that we call purpose for our organization—why we exist. We have also identified guiding principles (soft skills) that establish accountability for how we treat each other on this journey. For the leader and their team, we have tried to remove subjectivity and a moving target for what success looks like. We've leveraged our destination to tell us what to do next and who will do it.

Alignment isn't a one-time exercise; we must align and be aligned every single day. Misalignment is the natural flow of most human interaction. You have to fight—every moment of every day—to be aligned to your people so they have a chance at true fulfillment. For most people, success is circumstantial, so don't let the circumstances of each day create misalignment. Instead, leverage each circumstance to deepen the bonds of trust so that success can be more tangible for all on the journey.

Don't let your people's hard work and dedication go to waste and create a false sense of success. Stay aligned. No matter what. **Alignment is a requirement of fulfillment.**

Dream a Little

In step three, we talked about creating value in your employees by recognizing, celebrating, and leveraging their soft skills and passions. Hopefully you see them differently now and you truly value your people for who they are (soft skills and passions) and not what they can do. This process of creating value in your people will also yield a great amount of trust. We now need to leverage that trust to get your people to start dreaming about their future. I know, this might sound weird. I am telling you though, most human beings never get the chance to acknowledge, let alone *talk* about, their dreams. In fact, depending on their worldview, they might not even give themselves permission to dream. Reimagining the future will forever change the course of someone's life in ways we can't imagine.

Pursue your people and do it on purpose. Take the time to truly understand how your people envision the future. One way to talk about the future with your people is through the lens of a career path. Your job, as the leader, is to anticipate based on the value of your people what this path might look like. This way, you can dream about what they might be doing down the road together. For most employees, a tangible aspect of determining their career path is by understanding how their boss values their current performance ... their future often rests on how well their annual performance review turns out. You can see why this causes a lot of anxiety for most employees. Get this part right and you can start to unlock the future for your people.

The Dreaded Annual Performance Review

Like most bosses, I have given out a lot of annual performance reviews. It may not have elicited the same level of dread as it did for the employee, but I dreaded giving them, nonetheless. Why? Because I felt like a fraud. But it gave me a chance to talk about aspects of the employee— production, behavior, personality—that I avoided for most of the year. I also had no basis for the way I valued them. No predefined, objective target for them to hit.

These annual performance reviews also helped determine the employee's compensation for the upcoming year. I will always remember one specific performance review because it was so cringe-worthy. Our performance review system would produce a number from one to five that would be used to determine a potential raise. After filling out the performance review, someone received a score of 3.9. When I met with the employee and went through the review, I realized that a 3.9 missed out on the highest potential raise by 0.1. After seeing the disappointment in her face, what did I do? I gave her a 4.0 anyway. What was the point of going through this entire exercise with this employee only to make an arbitrary change based 100 percent on subjectivity? Why did I make her suffer through the indignity of being just a number?

Sound familiar? Some employees like this process. They're desperate for *any* feedback. And while the typical annual performance review leaves a lot to be desired, at least it's something. As a leader, the concept of "at least" should never enter into our thinking. Loving and serving your people toward fulfillment requires way more than "at least."

Whatever form of performance review you're going to use must remove all subjectivity. You have to decide ahead of time, with your people, how you will grade their performance. The concepts in this book are specifically designed to force your feedback to be through the lens of objectivity. Remember, you don't want a moving target for your people. Subjectively rating your employees based on your mood, poor communication, irritating personalities, or, even worse, bias or prejudice is why good people leave. The natural response to this typical process is to leave both parties frustrated, disappointed, and let down.

The idea of reviewing the performance of your people through the lens of alignment is a good thing. Doing it rarely and subjectively is not. Hopefully you've seen that the process of aligning will force you to review their performance each week, day, and even hour.

Recognize Greatness

In traditional management, companies typically determine career paths by hard skill, personality, tenure, long hours, and even kissing up. This method devalues human beings. As you experience your people applying their value (soft skills and passion) to a purpose they believe in, you will start to look for ways to increase their influence in your team or organization. As you start to create value in your eyes around your people, you won't be able to stop yourself from imagining how they can play a bigger role in accomplishing your purpose.

Watching them apply their value as a human being to the purpose and guiding principles will lead you to see them for who they are—you will **recognize their greatness**. Once you see their greatness in action, you will start to imagine a career path that may, or may not, include your team or even the organization.

The biggest distraction in recognizing their greatness, ironically, will be work. Be steadfast. Persevere to stay present. Staying present will give you the best chance to be there when they start to believe in their greatness. I can tell you firsthand, it is one of the most fulfilling aspects of being a leader. To say it's rewarding is an understatement. It is the fuel that I need to help me keep pushing forward to align.

Fighting for their fulfillment, through alignment, builds an incredible trust. This trust will allow you to sit with your people and start to understand how they might envision their own future. As you discuss their value and, ultimately, their greatness, it will undoubtedly start to impact where they see themselves in the coming years. Make sure to bring them along in your vision for their future. Not only do they need to know how you see them today, but they need to start to believe in your version of their future. This gives you a chance to dream together—a chance to shape the future. Instead of worrying about their current job, or worrying about your current leadership, you get to dream together about both of your futures.

Fulfillment. This is how you love and serve your people toward their fulfillment. This is how, as a leader, *you* find fulfillment.

The concept of recognizing people's greatness is not concrete. It's an abstract understanding of how another human being provides value to your personal journey of transformation. In other words, you are not going to be able to read this chapter and then contend for someone's greatness without a determination to be a great, complete leader. In my next book, *Lead*, I will detail my personal journey of becoming a complete leader. My journey is far from over, but it has allowed me to not only recognize greatness in people but also to get a glimpse of my own greatness. I invite you to join me in being a complete leader so that we can truly create success for those we love.

Kyle's story has been a picture of this journey.

KYLE'S STORY: PART FOUR

Kyle had experienced firsthand what it meant to create value. This value was based on his soft skills and passions. Now, as a program director, Kyle was asked to take on a team of his own. He realized the importance of creating value for his own team.

With a determination to love and serve, Kyle helped shape success for his people through his daily celebration of their value. He recognized their greatness and established a deep trust with his team. They began to dream together and jump-start their own transformation. Once again, Kyle showed me the strength of his character in serving others. I needed him to lean in even further and asked him to be on my executive team, working directly alongside me.

After accepting, he told me that the first investment I made into him during his orientation experience had changed his life. No one had spoken value into him as a person as I had, and now he knew fulfillment was possible because of who he was. He had truly transformed through alignment and was even helping others transform and find fulfillment.

His wife, Jessica, later told me about the changes that took place at home as a result of what he learned. She saw a renewed confidence in him and a graceful intentionality in the way he communicated. He could better articulate his expectations for their relationship because he was no longer afraid to put himself out there. He wasn't perfect by any means, but experiencing the significance of investment himself motivated him to always put in the effort. He spent more time investing into her as a person and brought forth her value in who she was every day. He had grown as a person and realized how his words had power to speak value into others, both to those he worked with and his family at home.

That small investment I made back on his first day sparked his fulfillment and transformation. It really is that simple. Just little moments over time and dedication to the process became a catalyst for change. Because of his experience, Kyle found fulfillment in all areas of his life. But he's not done yet. Every day, I see him continuing to show others how to do the same. His value to me, his team, and my organization is not based on tasks he accomplished or keeping clients happy—it's based on who he is. I saw it that first day, and through continued investment, he found fulfillment.

Greatness

Greatness is the application
of people's value
toward a shared purpose.

WHAT'S NEXT?

I n sharing Kyle's story with you, I've shared one of my greatest achievements as a leader. These stories are why I transformed from an authoritative leader to a more empathetic, vulnerable, and transparent leader. Although my journey started in the workplace, that transformation carried over into my personal life as well. Remember that this is a journey, one that I'm still on and will continue for you. This transformation is not a place you arrive to; it's a constant pursuit.

When everything's going well at your company, everyone will be onboard with the culture (purpose and principles). They'll be happy to continue cultivating the culture and doing what they have agreed to do—what they want to do—to live out the purpose.

During tough times, they will be tested. Stress and crisis put a terrible strain on purpose and principles. They typically force leaders to abandon the culture they've worked so hard to cultivate.

This is when you have to rely on the process of alignment to see you through. It's gotten you this far and it will pull you through the darkest hours if you don't sacrifice all that you've done by giving in to stress.

Cling to your purpose and principles. These are the times when your people need you most and when you must call upon the motivation that made you a leader in the first place. It was never about promotions, prestige, or profit. You care about people, and as long as you continue to love and serve your employees toward their fulfillment, you will be the calm in the storm they need.

It's easy to lead when things are going well. It becomes very difficult when circumstances take place that threaten the culture of your business, and that's when you need leaders who can step up and lead in a way that points people back to culture built on a belief in the purpose and guiding principles of the company.

You can learn this. You can do this. You can lead in good times and bad. You may not be there yet, but you will be. Everything I've told you in this book can be learned by anyone. Everyone can lead. It takes time, effort, and commitment and requires transformation and evolution, but you can adapt to be a leader for anyone. Be the leader and the person you want to be, inspiring others to be their best, most fulfilled selves.

There is only one foundational requirement for leadership, and that's to have a desire to love and serve your people. If you love your people, you'll be interested in discovering their passions and soft skills. You will care enough to invest in them, to figure out who they are and what they want. You'll appreciate them, value them, and work with them to figure out how they align with you and your company.

Hopefully, with this book, you've learned that *fulfillment* is not only possible, but that your people deserve *fulfillment*. Keep striving for the goal—to ensure that your employees have a chance at fulfillment. Continue to transform yourself as a leader and hold fast to what you've built. Don't lose sight of what you and your people have to gain.

Leadership becomes possible once you have alignment. This book was designed to show you a path to create alignment at work or home. Now that you have some level of alignment, you can start the process to develop leadership skills that will allow you and your team to thrive. No one is born a natural leader. It requires a determination to love and serve people toward fulfillment. We want to leverage that determination to discipline ourselves to be the best version of leadership we were made to be.

In my next book, *Lead*, I will be teaching you three leadership disciplines that have contributed to my transformation as a leader. You have a limited amount of time, words, and actions. I will show you how to use those three resources to become a complete leader.

Never stop pursuing your personal fulfillment. Fulfillment is the antidote for regret, so it's worth it!

Simple, Not Easy

This is simple, not easy. But by reading this book, you're already walking the path of transformation because of who you are. You have what it takes to be the leader that your people need—one that loves and serves their people toward fulfillment.

The journey toward transformation is just that—a journey—and it doesn't have an arrival; it's a constant, ongoing process. Allow yourself to be transformed and you'll have the ability to transform others.

I know this all feels daunting and overwhelming. You might be thinking, "How do I actually do this?" or even, "What if I don't do this?" You want to love and serve your people toward fulfillment, but in a world that believes in authority and achievement, how is it possible to invest in your culture?

Because I believe in this wholeheartedly, I've multiplied this philosophy into a consultation company that supports leaders and ultimately helps change the world by investing into organizations and leaders like you every day. I'd love to help you on your journey too!

ACKNOWLEDGMENTS

M y professional journey to where I am today started with my parents. I witnessed their dedication and diligence firsthand. They modeled what hard work can yield. They also gave me a shot in our little startup over twenty years ago. I am forever grateful for their gamble on me.

Along the way, I had the privilege of working with two men who forever influenced my life: Steve Courter and Jason Perkins. Steve showed me what compassion, humility, and sacrifice look like and selflessly gave his best for his family and friends. Jason taught me the power of unity. The concepts of purpose and guiding principles were born from his passion to unite people toward a common goal. Their investment in me has forged a lifetime of influence, and I can't ever thank them enough.

Currently, I've surrounded myself with seven remarkable human beings: Tabbatha Callaway, Ally Kauffman, Hayden Reid, Jaclyn Haertner, Emily Blanco, Lauren Spaulding, and Kyle Watson. Each one has had an impact on who I choose to be every day. I try to be better for them tomorrow because of their investment in who I am today. I'm thankful to each of you for pushing me to be the best version of myself.

I want to especially recognize those who made this book a reality. Emily Blanco was handed the task of getting this project off the ground and did so relentlessly. She persevered through the fear of the unknown and the fear of failure. Jaclyn Haertner stepped in to bring this all home. Her passion for the purpose of the book allowed what Emily started to come to fruition. Tabbatha Callaway poured her personal mission to positively impact lives into every word of this book. She stood by me through all the ups and downs and provided confidence, reflection, comfort, celebration, and pure passion. Jordan LeCroy coordinated the book's journey with enthusiasm and loyalty. I knew my heart would be followed through these words because she was committed to having my voice heard. Finally, I want to thank Lauren Spaulding and Kenzie Radke for their dedication to the evolution of the ideas in this book. Thank you all for your passion for this philosophy in order to bring this book to life.

I also want to thank our Alignment Leadership team, who helped bring practical application to the story that I'm telling through Alignment Leadership. I know they will continue to bring my vision of Alignment Leadership to the companies and individuals they interact with and ultimately ensure that my children experience fulfillment in the workplace.

Lastly, I'm grateful for my wife, who has been by my side for nearly thirty years. She prefers to be behind the scenes, but I could not be the man I am or, more importantly, the man I *want* to be without her. She tames my spirit at the end of each day, waits patiently for me to come back to the earth, endures my wild ideas, and loves me for who I am. I will be better for you because you are better for me. Thanks for seeing me through it all.

ABOUT THE AUTHOR

Chris Meroff has found his leadership purpose and he wants to help you find yours.

Libraries of leadership books have been written.

Chris has probably read most of them. He would be the first to tell you that his own leadership journey has had its share of ups and downs. But there is a lot to be learned from failure, and, thankfully, he has gained great wisdom and made important discoveries that are changing the lives of those he leads every day.

He has figured out that the true definition of leadership is "loving and serving those you lead to fulfillment." That's a huge undertaking and not one to be taken lightly. Pizza parties and bowling nights can be a part of that process, but in Alignment Leadership, there is so much more. The conversations are more and deeper. The depth of relationship is more. The sacrifices made for each other is more. Most importantly, the people he leads are finding their calling and place in this world, and they are doing more than they could ever have imagined. It is nothing short of a revolution.

And so, Chris is adding his own work to that leadership library. This is book one in a three-part series that will teach you as a leader how to *Align*, *Lead*, and *Thrive*. His hope is that you will take these concepts and build a great culture built on love and respect and that you and your team will do more in this world and become all that you were intended to be.

Chris lives in Austin, Texas with his wife, Sue. They have four grown children, Ben, Liz, Grace, and Josh.

CPSIA information can be obtained
at www.ICGtesting.com
Printed in the USA
JSHW021914100221
11792JS00001B/21